ROMAN BRITAIN

I. A. RICHMOND

PENGUIN BOOKS

Penguin Books Ltd, Harmondsworth, Middlesex
U.S.A.: Penguin Books Inc., 3300 Clipper Mill Road, Baltimore 11, Md
AUSTRALIA: Penguin Books Pty Ltd, 762 Whitehorse Road,
Mitcham, Victoria

—

First published 1955
Reprinted 1958

Made and printed in Great Britain
by Hunt, Barnard & Co, Ltd
Aylesbury

CONTENTS

LIST OF ILLUSTRATIONS

LIST OF PLATES

LIST OF FIGURES

EDITORIAL NOTE

Roman Britain is the first volume of a series planned to form an intelligent and consecutive guide to the development of English Society in all its aspects from the Roman invasion to the outbreak of the First World War. Each volume has been written by a specialist, and each author has been left to decide what he himself considers significant and interesting in the period with which he deals, and to make his own balance between the claims of the sub-divisions of his general thesis, politics, economics, culture, religion, social life, colonial expansion, foreign relations. All have sought to emphasize the sense of period, and while some parallels are inevitable, the business of discovering comparison and conclusion, and of adapting the lessons of history to our own times, is left, for the most part, to the reader.

As in Professor Richmond's *Roman Britain* the evidence for his conclusions is based rather more on archaeological than on documentary sources, the publishers have taken the step of asking the author to include in this volume a number of illustrations.

The complete work consists of eight volumes, as follows:

1. ROMAN BRITAIN. *By Professor Ian Richmond,* King's College, Newcastle-on-Tyne.
2. THE BEGINNINGS OF ENGLISH SOCIETY (FROM THE ANGLO-SAXON INVASION). *By Dorothy Whitelock,* Fellow of St Hilda's College, Oxford.
3. ENGLISH SOCIETY IN THE EARLY MIDDLE AGES. *By Doris Mary Stenton,* Lecturer at Reading University.
4. ENGLAND IN THE LATE MIDDLE AGES. *By A. R. Myers,* Lecturer at Liverpool University.
5. TUDOR ENGLAND. *By S. T. Bindoff,* Professor of History at Queen Mary College, London.
6. ENGLAND IN THE SEVENTEENTH CENTURY. *By Maurice Ashley,* formerly Scholar of New College, Oxford.
7. ENGLAND IN THE EIGHTEENTH CENTURY. *By Dr J. H. Plumb,* Fellow of Christ's College, Cambridge.
8. ENGLAND IN THE NINETEENTH CENTURY (1815–1914). *By David Thomson,* Fellow of Sidney Sussex College, Cambridge.

J. E. MORPURGO

AUTHOR'S PREFACE

DURING this century the subject of Roman Britain has grown, and grown so large that all aspects of it cannot be covered in a small volume. Many, moreover, are aspects so technical as to demand more specialized treatment than is here appropriate. The choice of subject and treatment has therefore followed the author's own inclinations, dictated by the subjects upon which evidence rather than conjecture holds the field. For the use of those who would explore further a bibliography for each chapter is included, not in itself complete but sufficient to equip those who use it to the full to find the way about the subject for themselves.

I. A. R.

Newcastle upon Tyne, 1954

CHAPTER ONE

MILITARY HISTORY

THE earliest political connexion of Rome with these islands came so suddenly that it was almost the first connexion of any kind between the Roman world and Britain. During the five years which preceded the invasion of Julius Caesar in 55 B.C. the Roman frontier had been advanced from the Alps and the Cevennes to the shores of the Channel: and, while there is evidence that in Gaul Roman merchants had for some time exploited the possibilities of trade in the areas then being occupied by Roman troops, there is no suggestion that they habitually crossed the sea to Britain. In contemporary literature knowledge of Britain is second-hand, derived ultimately from stray voyagers' accounts, garbled and misunderstood, or sometimes, as in the case of the best of all, disbelieved because the truth seemed stranger than fiction. Roman public opinion felt distant Britain as almost legendary, the source of mineral wealth, its very size and definition as an island in doubt, a new world of awesome isolation and uncharted risk. This explains the excitement with which Rome received the news of an invasion of Britain by Caesar and judged it an exploit of unexampled enterprise and daring, adding new laurels to him who had conceived it and new prestige to the name of Rome.

If this was the effect upon the Roman audience to which Caesar was playing, the effect at the scene of action was stunning. In two swift invasions in successive years Caesar had come and gone. Not scatheless; ignorance of the Channel tides twice took a heavy toll in ships, and

British chariot warfare proved disconcerting in its supple mobility. But not unrewarded; Cassivellaunus, the principal dynast of the south-east, had offered unconditional surrender; a powerful and friendly tribe, the Trinovantes of Essex, had accepted Roman protection; hostages had been given and taxes had been assigned. If the objective of the expedition was, as Caesar alleged, to prevent British powers from aiding the Gauls, then it might be considered amply achieved. If annexation was intended, the first steps had been taken, following which a definite occupation might later be planned.

It is well known that events took a different turn: Caesar's energies and ambition being diverted first by the Gallic revolt and presently by civil war; while Augustus, heir to his destiny but not to his temperament, cautiously built up a new political system which required so much consolidation as to encourage no cross-Channel venture. This time it was the Britons who were the distant political audience, and upon them the achievements of Augustus and his successors were not lost. There was no doubt, for Caesar had demonstrated this once and for all, that Britain lay within the Roman grasp: and all kinds of motives might set the military machine in motion: personal ambition, economic covetousness, or a political grievance. The two former were outside British calculation, but the last could be studiously avoided, the more so since Rome conveniently forgot to require Caesar's conditions of tribute. Meanwhile, there was the reality of the Roman export and import market, now brought within a fine day's view. This could provide a British chief with luxuries of a kind unobtainable elsewhere and highly appealing to an uninhibited sense of enjoyment, among the foremost being the luxuries of the table and imported wine. The new impulse given to trade is reflected by the widespread adoption of coinage on the Gallic model throughout south-eastern Britain, in those denominations of silver and gold which go with commercial interest in luxury articles only.

But the proximity of Rome had another social effect, apart from the allurements of high life. Tribal society, as conceived in Celtic terms, was not a democracy or a tyranny but an oligarchy, which took the form of government sometimes by a council of nobles and elected magistrates and sometimes by a king and his counsellors. In such states the presence of strong factional interests was inevitable, and it was natural that such factions should endeavour to enlist the favour or sanction of Roman support, in reality or pretence. The reigning faction would be anxious to assert its position, the exiled rival always hopeful that Roman support might be brought, or bought, to redress the balance. This explains alike the Latin legends and Roman political forms on the coinage of reigning dynasts or the appearance of British kings as suppliants of Augustus or worshippers of Jupiter Capitolinus. But it need not imply that the policy of such rulers conformed to the sanction which it invoked. There is, on the contrary, every indication that, apart from correct external relations with the great power, British dynasts went their own way. The most striking case of actual reversal of Roman policy is provided by the fate of the Trinovantes, whom Caesar had specifically protected against their powerful and aggressive neighbours, the Catuvellauni, of Hertfordshire and district. This did not save them from complete absorption by the Catuvellauni some fifty years later, a step which advanced Cunobelinus, the contemporary representative of the line of Cassivellaunus, to virtual suzerainty of south-eastern Britain. His realm seems to have embraced the Chilterns and the

middle Thames valley, as well as Essex and part of Kent.
The Trinovantian lands, however, were the richest, and
it was there that Cunobelinus established, about A.D. 10,
his new capital of Camulodunum at Colchester. By
Mediterranean standards the place was not a town at
all. It covered a huge area, twelve square miles enclosed by
great dykes, but habitations were concentrated in small
scattered units. Mercantile and productive activity lay,
as might be expected, along the riverside, and excavation
shows that overseas trade was brisk. Here were concentrated the moneyers, whose moulds, for silver blanks
which were to be struck as coins, themselves strike the
imagination by their crude ingenuity. Like most ancient
rulers, Cunobelinus used his coinage for self-advertisement. It records the name of his new capital, Camulodunum, 'the fortress of Camulos', the war-god whom the
Catuvellauni had brought with them to Britain from the
plains of north-eastern France and who had hewn them
out a fair heritage. But the most constant type is the
lovely reverse with the corn-ear, reminding us not only
that this was the natural product of Essex acres but that
the contemporary geographer Strabo mentions corn as
one of the principal British exports. 'Corn, cattle, gold,
silver, and iron', runs his list: 'these are brought from
Britain; also hides, slaves, and clever hunting-dogs'.
Minerals are not found in the territory of Cunobelinus;
he must have drawn his silver from Derbyshire or
Somersetshire and his gold from further west. But the
other items in the list could all have figured among the
exports of his kingdom, and we get a picture of how the
imports of such a Celtic prince were balanced. The subject Trinovantes would produce the corn, the middle
Thames and the Chilterns the cattle, the forests the hides
and pelts, the aristocratic kennels the hunting dogs. The

slaves form a darker picture, recalling the fact that no neighbours of a thriving native kingdom were exempt from slave-raiding and head-hunting, accepted respectively as the profit and proof of martial prowess. The imports were numerous. Wine, represented by the great containers of coarse pottery in the tombs of native noblemen silver table-ware and bronze-plated furniture from the same sources; fine pottery from Italy; and from southern and north-eastern Gaul can be reckoned as tangible proof. Strabo mentions in particular ivory, jewellery, and glass. But there must have been much else of frailer constitution which has not survived. The tale is rounded off by two specially significant objects from the Essex area. Amid the burnt remains of a princely cremation at Lexden, near Colchester, was found a carefully mounted medallion of Augustus, which had been cast on to the pyre with other particularly valued possessions of the dead nobleman. The mounting is Roman, and the whole object is evidently a special present from the Roman world and of official import, precisely comparable with the portrait of King or Queen treasured by a paramount chief. No less remarkable is the little portrait bust of the Emperor Gaius (Caligula) from Colchester: nobody valued the memory of this mad and capricious ruler after his death, and the bust acquires meaning only as a contemporary token of regard by a philo-Roman notable at a time when Roman intervention was fully expected.

In other areas of the island changes which took place between the days of Caesar and Augustus were much less propitious. King Commius of the Gallic Atrebates, once the trusted emissary of Caesar to British kings, broke altogether with Rome after the great revolt of 53–52 B.C. and fled overseas to Britain. It may be presumed that he and his followers were the principal figures in the tribe of British Atrebates, and his descendants are later found issuing coins spread over Surrey and Kent. The example of flight from Caesar's wrath was followed by many, high and low, from north-western Gaul, where the vengeful hand of Caesar fell heaviest. For them the easiest land-fall was the coast of Dorsetshire and Hampshire, long open to cross-Channel commerce. They found there a culture and people akin to their own, but here too the newcomers brought new names. It is not clear that they were responsible for the name Durotriges, applied to the folk of Dorset; but they certainly gave the name Belgae to the tribe centred in Wiltshire, borrowing for a single unit formed of various immigrant communities the name once famous in Gaul as that of a ferocious confederacy of tribes, noted for their savagery and independence. Their cultural equipment reflects their mixed origins, but they found and developed an art of fortification already intro-duced to the area from their old homeland by way of the south-west. This was the defence in depth, with massive rampart, multiple ditch, and barbican gateways. These fortifications, the strongest and most complex that Britain had yet known, were needed to overawe subject popula-tions and to defy potential rivals. In this respect the war-rior chiefs must have resembled the Norman overlords of a later age with their new-fashioned castles and their retainers. What they lacked was the common overlord to whom fealty was due.

Amid this strife and commotion, which meant a grim fate for the conquered or dispossessed, it is not surprising that few other stable communities emerge in south-eastern Britain. For some time after the reign of Augustus southern Surrey and Sussex appear to have been the dominion of one Verica, of the lineage of Commius, whose coinage displays the vine-leaf as its outstanding emblem. This ought to mean that, just as Cunobelinus extolled the wheat-ear as the basis of his commercial prosperity, so Verica owed much to the vine or its products. Verica, like both his elder brothers, Eppillus and Tincommius, uses on his coinage the title *rex*, which implies either Roman recognition or the desire for it: and that explains why, when he was driven out of his kingdom shortly before A.D. 43, he should have gone overseas to appeal to Rome. Verica's expulsion seems to represent the final and most successful drive of Cunobelinus and his sons towards the south. In the Thames valley the struggle had been in progress, with varied success, for a generation and more; and this rivalry also had brought about the appearance of British suppliant kings at the court of Augustus. If Roman poets sometimes indulged in prophetic visions of a conquest of Britain, the island chieftains already viewed the event as a sobering likelihood.

None of the kingdoms so far described lay further than fifty or sixty miles from the coast, and all were clustered about Britain's continental front. Behind them lay older-established tribes, whose aristocratic families may indeed have included younger adventurers from the world which we have been describing but whose peoples had no reason to welcome the aggressive warrior kingdoms established on their borders. Such were the Dumnonii of Cornwall and Devon, the Dobunni of Somerset and Gloucestershire, the Coritani of Leicestershire and Lincolnshire, and the Iceni of Norfolk. The Dumnonii, rich in mineral resources, had as yet developed no coinage, a sure indication of backward commercial development. The Coritani seem to have used the coinage of their more powerful neighbours, if at all. Only the Dobunni and Iceni coined in abundance, but in very conservative style, unmarked by inventiveness or originality. Wealth there was, and artistic talent to serve it, as is shown by the lovely mirrors and chariot-furnishings or, in a lesser field, the decorated pottery: and Roman products reached the area also, if in a thinner stream. Here was a sphere much less pervious to Roman influences; partly because its own civilization was set and firm, partly because relations with the coast-ward tribes through which such influences must pass were bad, and partly because the coastward tribes were themselves absorbing the market. When the time came, these districts were to be among the most Romanized in Britain: for the moment they were cut off from the new civilization by hostility, greed, and lack of enterprise.

Beyond them again lay the mountain or forest tribes. In Wales, the Romans were to come to know two as formidable enemies; the Silures of Monmouthshire and Glamorganshire, and the Ordovices of Powys. Covetous of their richer neighbours of the plain, these tribes had somehow made contact with the kingdom of Cunobelinus, probably through their mineral wealth. The third Welsh tribe, the Deceangli of Flintshire, also famous for minerals, were an easy prey to Roman aggression when the time came. The relations of the Coritani, of Shropshire and Cheshire, are less certain. Their hill-fortresses were systematically dismantled by Rome in later days, and it may thus be presumed that they were regarded as actively or potentially hostile. Next came the Brigantes, a very large but loosely knit tribe, covering most of the six northern counties: 'numerically the largest tribe in Britain,' writes Tacitus, but of unreliable political stability, as the Romans were later to learn to their cost. Finally, the Parisi of east Yorkshire complete the outer fringe. These folk, like the Catuvellauni of Hertfordshire, had come from the north-eastern plains of Gaul, bringing with them a rich civilization of magnificent war-chariots, armour, and accoutrements. Once established in east Yorkshire, the tribe had swarmed: and their rich and characteristic armour or weapons can be traced through west Yorkshire to Cumbria, Galloway, and even Northern Ireland. It is clear that the aristocratic culture of the whole north must owe much to these pushful and restless adventurers. Those who stayed in east Yorkshire were of more settled nature. Before the Claudian conquest they were already welcoming Roman and Trinovantian products to trading stations on the Humber.

Almost a century elapsed between the invasion of Caesar in 55 B.C. and the conquest of Britain by Claudius in A.D. 43. The contrast in the political situation was enormous. In Caesar's time only a corner of south-eastern Britain was within purview. The south-west was closed and hostile, the interior impenetrable to inquiry owing to its bitter hostility to the tribes of the south-east. Before the Claudian invasion, the *pied-à-terre* gained by Roman merchants had widened into a vast sphere of influence. Their products had reached the Humber, Trent, and Severn and their knowledge of lands and peoples beyond this may well have been less vague than Caesar's knowledge concerning southern Britain. When the Claudian invasion came the responsible staff was able to draw its intelligence from a far wider and better informed circle of traders and merchants than had been available a century earlier, and there were exiled dynasts whose political information must have been both precise and valuable.

It will be evident that in Britain itself the possibility of Roman intervention in the affairs of the island had long been expected before the immediate causes of the event came about. These were themselves various: as in many

political events, no single cause can be regarded as exclusively operative. First, there was the expulsion by
Cunobelinus of his son Adminius, who fled overseas and
made an act of submission to the Emperor Gaius in
A.D. 40. This appeal had coincided with the mounting of
an expeditionary force by Gaius, which never got further
than Boulogne, owing to other preoccupations. A year or
two later came the death of Cunobelinus, the division of
his kingdom between Togodumnus and Caratacus, and
the encroachment upon the kingdom of Verica, who fled
to Claudius. With the exiled princes had no doubt gone
other notables, and it was then that the Britons, having
claimed extradition of the exiles in vain, made the foolish
mistake of creating disturbances on the Gallic coast. This
is the meaning of the laconic phrase of Suetonius, '*tumultu-
antes Britannos ob non redditos transfugas*'.

The military problem set by the disorders on the Gallic
coast now began to take shape. If Britain were not to be
absorbed in the Empire and were left to become anti-
Roman with impunity, then the creation of an Atlantic
frontier would be a necessity. This was not in itself
impossible, since it would have perhaps demanded no
more men than went to garrison Britain. But it was
fiscally less advantageous, since it threw the burden of
an extra garrison on to an Empire no bigger than before:
in other words, the costs of an army against Britain were
not to be offset by the revenues of a conquered Britain.
Again, it would disturb the balance built up between the
army commanders of the Danube and the Rhine, by
placing in north-western Europe forces which out-
weighed any others within striking distance of Italy and
the centre of Empire. This ran counter to the delicate
statecraft of Augustus, who owed his power to an equili-
bration of his chief army commands, each the sphere of a

Figure 1

potential rival, and left the principle as a political legacy cherished by his successors. On the other hand, if the extra power were placed overseas, literally isolating it in an island-province, whence it could not return except by suborning a fleet subjected to a separate command, this measure would leave the Continental position very much as before and would thus solve both the fiscal question and the political problem at once.

The troops selected for the occupation were four legions, the Second Augusta, previously stationed on the Upper Rhine at Strasbourg, the Ninth Hispana from Pannonia, the Fourteenth Gemina from the Middle Rhine at Mainz, and the Twentieth Valeria Victrix from the Lower Rhine at Neuss. They were accompanied by many auxiliaries, including not a few Gallic and Thracian regiments. But the start was not auspicious. The soldiery, acutely disturbed by what seemed like banishment to another world, refused to embark, and only the arrival of a freedman as special commissioner from Rome brought them back to their duty in a tumultuous burst of self-respect. The time required for a report to Rome and for the despatch of such a commissioner implies that the mutiny lasted not less than a month, and in one respect it served its authors well. The Britons, thinking that the outcome would be the postponement or abolition of the invasion, maintained no force to oppose the landing. Disembarkation and consolidation of a great maritime stores-base at Richborough (Rutupiae) were carried out unhindered. To save time and to distract resistance, which the Romans had expected, the forces had landed at three different points, presumed to be the natural harbours of Dover (Dubrae) and Lympne (Lemanae), as well as the main landing point on Thanet. Room for deployment was thus secured.

The Britons now rallied, depending as of old upon their tactical skill in chariot warfare. The leaders of the British forces were Togodumnus and Caratacus, but they depended too much upon natural obstacles and too little upon their power of manoeuvre, thoroughly underrating the ingenuity and resource of Roman troops in the face of river-crossings. At the first pitched battle, on the Medway, the Roman auxiliary troops crossed and caught the charioteers off their guard, and in the two-day battle which followed, Vespasian, commander of the Second Legion, achieved a successful surprise attack, while Hosidius Geta won a resounding victory by firmly sustained pressure and bold personal risk. The next river was the Thames itself, across which the Britons retreated without arranging for an effective rearguard action and allowed their retreat beyond the river to be cut off by Roman troops who had crossed uncontested, even using a bridge. The lack of counsel here displayed was no doubt due to the previous death of Togodumnus: and it is the more readily explicable when it is realized that, on the death of Cunobelinus, Togodumnus had taken the old kingdom, in Essex and Hertfordshire, while Caratacus had taken the westward kingdom of the middle Thames, Hampshire, and Surrey. Thus, on defeat at the Medway, the Britons must in fact have split into two groups, one retreating westward under Caratacus, the other, leaderless, making headlong for home to north of the river. For nine long years Caratacus was to be a thorn in the side of the Roman army in Britain and was to gain many successes, some cheap and others dear: but history tells of his fighting only one more pitched battle, on ground of his own choice, when he risked all and lost all in a final and crushing defeat.

The way to Camulodunum lay wide open, but Aulus

Plautius, commander-in-chief of the expedition, chose now to halt at the Thames and to await the arrival of Claudius. The moment had come for which Claudius himself must have longed, when he could add a new province to the Empire, leading his army in triumph to the native capital and gaining thereby a success worthy of his long line of distinguished ancestors. The pride of the Claudian family was proverbial, but in this representative it was perhaps pardonable, for to him success in life had come so unexpectedly and so late. The ambition to add lustre to the Claudian name was certainly matched by a desire to obliterate from memory the nugatory performances of Gaius in this very theatre of war and so to uphold the reputation and glory of Rome. These motives too must certainly be taken into account in any assessment of the causes of the British war. Nor was the share of Claudius in the war wholly negligible. He himself took command of the advance beyond the Thames, fought a pitched battle with the natives, and then entered the royal city of Cunobelinus in triumph: and history records that other exploits, packed into a sixteen-day campaign, forced unnamed tribes into surrender. Two further scraps of information have come down to us. Other tribes were already voluntarily making their submission; and the Roman Senate, abrogating its constitutional right to ratify treaty terms, announced its willingess to accept as valid, agreements concluded on the spot by Claudius or his legates.

Among the earliest of the native potentates to ask for a treaty was Cogidumnus, who inherited the kingdom of Verica, in Sussex. The value of his adhesion to the Romans was considerable, for it gave them a needed springboard for the next stage in the conquest, the attack upon the Durotriges and Belgae of Dorsetshire and Wiltshire. As a reward for his services Cogidumnus received at least two other tribes as subjects, and the unique title of *rex et legatus Augusti in Britannia*, marking him at once as a native prince and a Roman official, whose sphere was extra-territorial to the rest of the province. When he died, the arrangement did not continue: but the memory of it lived on in the name of his people, the Regnenses, or people of the native kingdom (*regnum*). Another native potentate, famed far and wide for his wealth, was quick to secure it by rapid submission. This was Prasutagus, king of the Iceni of Norfolk, whose friendship was also welcome because it secured the right flank of the Roman advance. But his subsequent record was less satisfactory than that of Cogidumnus, whose reputation for loyalty was of the highest. When the moment for disarmament came, about four years later, Prasutagus did not carry all his people with him and a large resistance group had to be drastically repressed by Roman arms, for the move-ment was spreading to other tribes.

Meanwhile, Vespasian, whom fate was ultimately to make Emperor, was occupied in mounting the offensive against the west. It is unfortunate that for the account of these operations we have to depend entirely upon secon-dary sources. No names are given, except that of the Isle of Wight (Vectis), which was reduced to unconditional surrender. The biographer of Vespasian speaks only of two very strong tribes and the capitulation of over twenty native fortresses (*oppida*). The two very strong tribes can hardly be other than the Durotriges and Belgae, and, if so, the fortresses lay in Dorset and Wiltshire. Two Dorset hill-forts have furnished to archaeology dramatic evi-dence of their fate. The first, Maiden Castle, of which the native name was Dunum (the fortress, *par excellence*), is the biggest of all. In its final form, as seen to-day, it is still

vastly impressive. Two immense ditches form the outer
defences of two huge ramparts while the main entrance
is complicated by a double horn-work. The Romans had
these obstacles to face also: but they saw them crowned
with stockades and rendered sheer in stone and timber,
while the gates were blocked with massive doors and
overshadowed by great towers, as excavation has shown.
But excavation also revealed an emergency cemetery
within the hornworks, where the dead were hastily
interred during the Roman assault. The skeletons bear
evidence of the murderous effect of the Roman weapons.
The slashing cuts from the auxiliaries' swords, the stabs
from the legionaries' cut-and-thrust or the deadly little
square hole drilled in the skull by their throwing-spear
(*pilum*), the bolt from a field gun which stuck fast in a
spinal column: all attest the heavy fighting inexorably
pushed home which won for Vespasian his military
reputation. The anklets and toe-rings of the dead, on the
other hand, are the personal adornments of savages, the
manner of men who had to be faced. Discoveries of this
kind almost lift the veil of the centuries.

The second site is Hod Hill, north-east of Blandford.
Systematic excavation is now in progress and its results
cannot be anticipated: but on the ground the hand of
Rome is self-evident. One corner of the not irregular hill-
fort which crowns a bold plateau is cut off by the truly
regular lines of a Roman fort, for some time the quarters
of a legionary detachment and some cavalry. What happened here is clear enough. While at Maiden Castle,
after surrender, a remnant of the inhabitants were allowed
to use the dismantled fortress and to live within its bounds,
at Hod Hill the fortress, whether emptied of inhabitants
or not, received a garrison. This marks a difference in
treatment, and so it ultimately worked out. In the neigh-

bourhood of Maiden Castle, on the site of the modern
Dorchester, there was to grow up the modest Romanized
capital of the Durotriges, amid a district full of well-to-do
landowners. Hod Hill, on the other hand, is the south-
western gateway to Cranborne Chase: and this remained
a land of native farmers, consistently kept for generations
at a uniformly low level of existence, like *fellahin*. Unconditional surrender here brought in its train not freedom
but misery, and the legionary garrison was there to
enforce its first organization, until the inmates of this
special enclave had passed from subjects to serfs.

Just as the removal of the menace represented by the
kingdom of Cunobelinus secured for the conqueror the
friendship of those tribes which had once feared it, so in
the west the conquest of the Durotriges and the Belgae
brought new accessions of allies, or tribes in treaty relation. Foremost among these were the Dumnonii and the
Dobunni. The former needed from Rome little but the
advantages of peaceful intercourse. The latter, on the
other hand, required Roman protection from their wilder
neighbours in the Welsh hills and forests, and it was on
the western fringe of their territory, at the Severn crossing
of Gloucester (Glevum), that the first standing legionary
fortress of the south-west was established. How matters
stood further north-east is uncertain. The loyalty of communities bordering upon the Iceni was very soon found
to be shaky, and it may therefore have been a demand
for precaution rather than protection which induced the
Roman high command to quarter among the Coritani
the Ninth Legion at Lincoln. At this end of the frontier,
screened by Severn and Trent, which was thus being
almost automatically roughed out, the northward thrust
secured or brought about an arrangement of great
political importance. The very large canton of the

Brigantes, which embraced the entire northern front, entered into treaty relations with Rome through their Queen Cartimandua. The reason is not far to seek. During the next twenty years there were to be many proofs that this tribe in particular was prey to bitter partisan quarrels, in which its royal family took a leading part. The object of the alliance was thus to strengthen the queen's hand, and her action in A.D. 51, of delivering Caratacus into Roman hands after he had come within her grasp, shows her anxiety to insure with Rome rather than to honour a claim working against her inclinations. But for the moment the alliance was of immense value to Rome, since it guaranteed comparative quiet on the northern front, and might seem for the future to promise that Roman garrisons need never penetrate the grim and profitless uplands beyond the Humber. Above all, it gave opportunity to wrestle with the problems presented by Wales.

The earlier dealings of the Roman high command with Wales seem at this distance of time to have been marked by a failure to view the problem as a whole. So far as any policy can be detected, the Roman plan seems to have been to deal with the tribes piecemeal, facing each problem as it presented itself: a plan without finality, which tended too often to leave the initiative in enemy hands. Many of the early ventures, too, were doomed to frustration or disappointment. The campaign of Ostorius Scapula in A.D. 49 against the Deceangli of Flintshire was robbed of its intended results by a disturbance among the Brigantes, which called for Roman armed intervention. Indeed, the two events may well have been connected; for the effect of subduing the Deceangli would have been to drive a wedge in between the unconquered Britons of the west and the north, a threat perhaps resented by the anti-Roman party among the Brigantes. Nor were the strategical implications of the situation unappreciated in other quarters. The next offensive by Ostorius was against the Silures, with whom Caratacus had found a refuge and an ideal terrain for guerilla warfare. The interpretation of the situation by Caratacus is clear from the action which he took. A British victory might enable him to keep the Roman forces out of Wales for longer: but a defeat might result in an immediate closing of the route of escape to the north. This explains why Caratacus moved his field of operations from the Silures to the Ordovices of Powys, and determined to put the issue to the test in a pitched battle, after which, if matters went ill, retreat to the north was still possible. The battle was a complete failure: despite the careful choice of very advantageous ground, the Britons were outmanoeuvred and outfought, ejected from their chosen positions and temporary fortifications by the superior discipline and equipment of the Roman troops. Caratacus escaped, but his family did not, and he himself made the fatal mistake of putting himself in the power of Queen Cartimandua of the Brigantes. The previous disciplinary measures and the present victory of Ostorius convinced the queen that duty and expediency coincided. Caratacus was trapped and delivered to the Romans in chains.

The Silures, however, continued to defy Roman attempts to penetrate their territory, cutting off auxiliary cohorts and harassing legionaries. For the time being they had to be contained and no attempt seems to have been made to penetrate the territory of the Ordovices either. Once again the Brigantian client kingdom re-quired attention. Cartimandua and her consort, Venu-tius, began an armed quarrel, in which Venutius was able to summon powerful external help. To restore order and induce a reconciliation Roman intervention with both auxiliaries and legionaries was required, without by any means immediate success. The shape of things to come was now beginning to emerge. The Trent-Severn frontier was not to provide the answer to the British political problem: instability among the Brigantes and downright hostility in Wales would demand the annexation and policing of much wider areas.

The next military operation on the Welsh front was one of singular interest. The governor of A.D. 59, Suetonius Paulinus, was a seasoned campaigner in Africa, where his chief exploit had been to defeat the tribes of the Atlas mountains by striking at the more distant plainlands from which they were fed and reinforced. In mountainous Wales, resistance was similarly nourished from the isle of Anglesey, populous, hospitable to refugees, and the seat of a large community of Druids, fanatically antagonistic to Rome. The recent discovery of a great hoard of objects, either devoted or destroyed but in any case certainly belonging to the priestly community, has shown how far their connexions ranged. The objects may have come as offerings or as tithes of booty – they are all war material, including the chains of captives: but they represent the spoils or riches of districts extending from south-west Britain to Yorkshire and even to Northern Ireland, represented by war-trumpets. Tacitus is so preoccupied with the dramatic contrasts of the situation that he does not quite clearly evaluate the connexion between the Druids and the political side of the picture. In fact, it becomes clear that Paulinus was not only wiping up a focus of material resistance but wiping out a native cult of which the influence was much more pervasive than any ancient author hints. It was one of the rare native cults with which the Roman government would make no compromise; not so much because of its tenets, which were not devoid of interest to educated Romans, as because of its use of human victims for augury and sacrifice. The expedition was carefully prepared, with landing-craft suited to the shallows of the Menai Strait, and the result was decisive. Just for a moment the attacking legionaries and auxiliaries, to whom magic and spells were a vivid everyday reality, stood appalled at the sight of the defenders, backed by praying and cursing priests and accompanied by wild women devotees who ran amok with flaming torches. Faith and discipline then triumphed and the Roman battle-line pressed forward to victory. The island was garrisoned and the sacred groves syste matically felled. Copying the African campaigning, Paulinus should next have undertaken the reduction of the tribes whose source of supplies, propaganda, and encouragement was now extinguished. He was prevented from doing so by an unexpected rebellion.

During the winter of A.D. 60–61, or a little before it, King Prasutagus of the Iceni had died. As a Roman client-king, he could not legally bequeath the succession to anyone, but his renowned wealth he had divided, giving half to the Emperor and a quarter each to his two daughters. His widow, Boudicca, does not appear to have been a legatee. In the absence of a male claimant to the throne, the Romans did not nominate a client-queen, Cartimandua having already proved a liability rather than an asset: and, before absorbing the kingdom into the province, began to divide the legacy, at the hands of army officers and Treasury agents. A first step was a con-solidation of Imperial property, which involved the revocation of grants made by Claudius to tribal notables. The relatives of the royal family were also made guaran-tors for payments. The entire tribal aristocracy was thus alienated by being treated as newly-conquered subjects,

culminating in the scourging of Boudicca and the viola-
tion of her daughters. The result was a wholesale revolt,
and this spread to the neighbouring tribe of the Trinovantes.

The Trinovantian rebellion had a rather different
cause. It is clear that this territory had been from the first
treated as conquered soil, whose inhabitants were at the
mercy and unconditional disposal of Roman conquerors.
On the site of the old native capital at Camulodunum, in
A.D. 49–50, the Romans began to lay out a new provincial capital, peopling it with a strong body of army
veterans. This meant the perpetual confiscation not
merely of land for the town but also of a sizeable land-
holding for each veteran, the size relating to army rank
previously held. Nor was captive territory assured of legal
protection from still further land-grabbing by Roman
settlers once established. The establishment of a strong
nucleus of veteran settlers in order to provide a focus of
loyal citizens as an insurance against possible rebellions
was not the sole purpose of the new *colonia*, as such a
foundation was called. The new capital was to be a focus
of provincial loyalty to Rome, which expressed itself, in
the fashion of the age, in an Imperial cult dedicated to
the living Emperor Claudius. The cult was to be served
by a high priest and priestess chosen annually from the
native allied and subject tribes from among their aristocracy and its duties involved not merely the observance of
a calendared series of rites but the payment for attendant
festivities, shows, games, and musical or literary contests.
The expenditure involved might suit and even repay the
ambitious philo-Roman: others would grudge or resent
it, according as it hurt their sentiments or their pockets.
From the Roman point of view, it was the best method of
creating a united feeling of loyalty and of sublimating

tribal ambitions and rivalries, just as it was an admirable means of inculcating Roman ideals and culture. It had, moreover, succeeded well in Gaul, where, however, it took the place of an existing annual gathering and was a burden spread over a far larger number of communities. On the Trinovantes these burdens fell particularly heavily. Part of the tribe, presumably the people of Togodumnus and his estates, were being summarily ejected to make way for the *colonia* and its lands: part was attributed to the *colonia* for administration and a graded citizenship, and upon this would fall the burdens of priesthood and the like. Of the common folk, many were toiling in labour-gangs upon the building of the *colonia*, while others tilled the new estates for exacting ex-army veterans. It cannot be supposed that these victorious soldiers were the best representatives of Roman civilization: indeed, Tacitus does not mince words in describing their insulting arrogance and they have themselves left behind them a magnificent centurion's tombstone and some highly piquant caricatures in clay to remind us that in their own circles pomp and vanity were not unaccompanied by satirical insight.

The acts which aroused satire in the conquerors engendered bitter rage and humiliation in the conquered, and these in turn bred revolt. It is not surprising that the Trinovantes were ready to join the Iceni, and there were others whose adherence was secret and did not emerge in the form of communal action. The course of the revolt itself is clear. The first move of the rebels was against Camulodunum, where the building programme had concentrated upon the Temple of Claudius and a senate house and theatre rather than upon the fortifications which were to enclose them. All resistance was over in two days and the captives were butchered with merciless and inhuman cruelty, particularly those reserved for sacrifice in the sacred groves. The Ninth Legion, too late to save the *colonia*, was itself very severely handled: two thousand men were afterwards required to bring it up to strength, and only the cavalry succeeded in escaping. This failure allowed the revolt to spread. Paulinus himself reached London in time to take stock of the situation, but his main body of troops was far behind and he did not dare risk being trapped. He therefore regretfully but firmly abandoned both London and Verulamium, which soon perished in fire and slaughter behind him, and sought to concentrate his troops before dealing with the enemy. Word was sent southwestwards to the Second Legion to join him and this implies that a concentration was planned somewhere near the junction of the Fosse Way and Watling Street, the two lines of communication necessary to such a plan of action. But his hand was forced. The Second Legion failed to move because its acting-commander disobeyed orders: commissariat difficulties were also acute in the late spring or early summer. In the end Paulinus felt he could wait no longer, and chose a battle-ground which gave him the maximum advantage in the face of a developing attack. The Romans, barely ten thousand strong, with a mixed force comprising one legion, a detachment, and auxiliary infantry and cavalry, were gravely outnumbered. Even the British casualties were later estimated at about eight times the whole Roman strength. But the Britons were badly equipped and armed, undisciplined and untrained, dangerous perhaps only upon ground of their own choosing or in surprise attack: and their mood was over-confident – they had even brought with them their families in wagons to witness the expected victory. The Romans had now chosen the battle-ground, on terrain entirely favourable to their disciplined and deliberate manoeuvre with greatly superior arms and armour. The Roman wedge-formations, applied simultaneously at various points, with lancer-charges to break any nucleated resistance, threw the Britons into disorder and pinned them in a helpless mass against the wagon-lines with which they had blocked their own retreat. The battle degenerated into grim and pertinacious slaughter, in which the rebels paid in full for their atrocities, accomplished and intended. Boudicca fled, quickly to die either by taking poison or through illness, according to different accounts, and the Romans began a systematic wasting by fire and sword of rebels and waverers. In their plight the Britons had one powerful advocate on the winning side. The new procurator, or chief Treasury official, who could report independently to the Emperor, advocated milder treatment as a means to end resistance and censured Paulinus for the circumstances which had led to rebellion. No doubt he anticipated a severe shrinkage in revenue following the devastations: and his own department had been so shamefully to blame for corruption and mismanagement that it may have been well to direct attention elsewhere. But other factors must also be taken into account. The procurator was himself a provincial or North Italian, and had married the daughter of a Gallic aristocrat who had taken a leading part in implementing a liberal policy of the Roman government towards his own tribe after just such a revolt. Roman history presents no more illuminating example of the interaction of Roman and provincial feeling in the new world which was being created in Western Europe. The government took the hint, but handled the situation tactfully. A special commissioner was sent out to observe conditions and reported less severely. Suetonius, who deserved well for his handling of the crisis, whatever his attitude to the subjugated, was soon recalled and the province settled down to lick its sores under a milder governor. Only seven years were to elapse before civil war shook the entire Roman world, and imposed upon the victor the task of impressing the frontier lands with renewed proof of Roman vitality and power.

The Flavian dynasty was fortunate in its earlier governors of Britain. The first, Petilius Cerealis, who had been through the Boudiccan revolt as legate of the Ninth Legion, was a clear-headed and stalwart upholder of Roman liberal policy and a firm if trenchant general. The second, Iulius Frontinus, was a passionate believer in efficiency as the basis of the senatorial partnership in Imperial rule. The third, Iulius Agricola, new to the senate, invites criticism owing to the idealization bestowed upon him by his famous son-in-law, the historian Tacitus; but his shrewd competence and political common-sense is not obscured by the theme of dutiful senator and ogre-Emperor. The work of all three governors hangs together, for it is the rounding-off of the British frontier problem.

The logical order of conquest imposed by the geographical formation of Britain requires that the subjection of the north should be preceded by the conquest of Wales. In A.D. 71, however, political events determined that this order should be reversed. Until then, the main theatre of war had been the Welsh border. But amid the world-wide uncertainty caused by the civil war of A.D. 69–70 northern Britain became the scene of a breakdown in Roman frontier policy which called for immediate attention as soon as the central government was strong enough to authorize it. The new situation was due to the collapse of the Brigantian client-kingdom as an organized philo-Roman community.

Failing the central portion of the *Annals* of Tacitus, history is silent as to the circumstances in which the Brigantian realm had become a Roman client state. But the event had happened early, soon enough for Cartimandua the queen to demonstrate her loyalty by the extradition of Caratacus, in A.D. 51. Nor must it be forgotten that such an act of faith was needed: the Brigantes had already given trouble a year or two before, when Ostorius had attempted to cut the connexion between Wales and the north by absorbing the Deceangli of Flintshire. The diversion thus created had checked the Roman effort and had demanded direct interference, followed by executions and a general pardon, in Brigantia. Thrones of client-rulers had been declared vacant for less than this, and Cartimandua, in particular, had reason to lean upon Rome for support. When later organized as a Roman canton the Brigantes, numerically the biggest tribe in Britain, covered north and west Yorkshire, together with Lancashire, Westmorland, Cumberland, and County Durham. They may even have spread beyond the Solway, where the tribal boundaries are obscure. This great area, sundered by the Pennines and their spurs into numerous divisions, each large enough to maintain powerful war-bands, must always have owed its cohesion to mutual advantage and to local balances rather than to inflexible domination from a single centre: in other terms, Brigantian central power was an overlordship, embracing numerous powerful septs, rather than a direct and immediate autocracy. The ancient way of reinforcing such a suzerainty was by marriage alliances, and that is the characteristic which Tacitus emphasizes in his thumb-nail sketch of Cartimandua, declaring that she owed her power to aristocratic connexions. And when, not long before A.D. 57, Cartimandua quarrelled with her

consort Venutius, her first move was to capture his
relatives. The answer was the organization by Venutius
of an invasion from outside the canton, thus demonstrat-
ing for the first time known to us the potential weakness
of the kingdom and its liability to disruption. Powerful
Roman forces were required in order to restore order.
But the followers of Venutius were not themselves free
from inconstancy. It was his armour-bearer, in Celtic
society normally the son of a powerful vassal, whom
Cartimandua presently espoused, doubtless hoping thus
to swing the balance of power in her favour. Venutius
waited his moment and in A.D. 69–70 came the opportunity. The Roman world was torn with civil war, the
British legions divided in loyalty, the governor unable to
command them, action beyond the frontier apparently
out of the question. Once more external help was forth-
coming and Venutius invaded the Brigantian kingdom,
where revolt was rife. Cartimandua was reduced to
extremities and this time only rescued with difficulty by
Roman auxiliaries. The legions did not move and the
kingdom fell to Venutius.

This triumph of the anti-Roman party converted the
Brigantes from a friendly buffer-state into a hostile tribe.
Experience had in fact shown that Roman support could
not guarantee a client-ruler in undisturbed possession.
Accordingly, Vespasian's first act in Britain was to
appoint a new governor, Petilius Cerealis, whose earlier
legionary command had been at Lincoln, in direct contact with the disaffected area. The intention was thus
clear for all to see, and Cerealis lost no time in translating
it into action. The line of approach to Brigantian territory is fixed by the natural land-bridge of the Lincolnshire and Yorkshire Wolds. The Yorkshire end of the line
lay through the territory of the Parisi, which embraced

the East Riding. Archaeology shows that ever since the
Claudian conquest this tribal area had been receptive of
Roman goods, while the later history of the tribe under
Roman rule demonstrates that their political development was more primitive than that of many British communities. In their position, wedged between the Roman
frontier and the Brigantian client-state, their choice of
adherence to Rome can never have been in doubt, and
they now, as probably before, opened the gate to Brigantia for Roman armies. The steps of Cerealis can be traced,
first at Brough, on the north bank of the Humber, where
the modest tribal capital of Petuaria was later to rise;
then at Malton, a second important Parisian centre, from
which all parts of the Vale of York can rapidly be reached;
finally, at York, where a convenient moraine provides
an easy crossing of the wide and marshy valley and
whence there is a water-way to the sea. At York was now
stationed the Ninth Legion, so that a link with the
western legions was possible; for the Twentieth, then
commanded by Agricola, had its part to play in the conquest, now singly and now in unison. The Brigantes were
evidently assailed upon both flanks and Cerealis could
claim to have absorbed a large part of their territory by
direct conquest or by surrender. How far his forward
campaigning extended is not clear, but along one principal line of penetration it may be possible to trace his
steps. The modern main road from the Vale of York to
Carlisle follows in most places the line of its Roman pre-
decessor, which is earlier than the Roman north road
from Chester to Carlisle and can hardly be later than
Agricola. Earlier still – for one of them is obliterated by
the York-Carlisle road – come three marching-camps, big
enough to hold a legion and some cavalry and of an
individual yet similar design quite different from those

associated with Agricola's troops. It is not unreasonable to assign these three works, which cover the route from Stainmore to Carlisle, to the army of Cerealis and in particular the Ninth Legion. Driving thus for the Solway and perhaps beyond it, Cerealis was using an age-old line of cultural and economic penetration which had been the principal channel of Brigantian expansion. The amount of early pottery at Carlisle has been thought to suggest that the grip on the Eden crossing was already more than temporary, as if an advanced post here ensured the fulfilment of terms of peace. The depth of the drive was no doubt conditioned by the existence of those external anti-Roman allies upon whom Venutius had been able to call with such effect a year or two before.

A pause could now be made in the north until the conquest of Wales was completed, a task which fell to the next governor, Iulius Frontinus. History has not preserved the earlier details of this senator's career, so that it cannot be definitely shown that previous service in Britain had equipped him with a knowledge of the theatre of war. But the operations manifestly went with a swing, amid conditions much less favourable to their execution. The Silures beyond the Severn, secure in the shelter of the Forest of Dean and the foothills of the Black Mountains, had retaliated vigorously after the defeat of Caratacus in A.D. 51–52, and were thereafter contained rather than controlled. The refusal of the Second Legion to move to the aid of Paulinus in A.D. 61 must be connected with unwillingness to invite a Silurian stab in the back. Experience had in short shown that frontal penetration was on this frontier impracticable. Profiting by the example of Paulinus, Frontinus decided to use sea force and to occupy the rich and fertile sea-plain of Glamorgan. Once a foothold was here obtained the immediate result was the conquest of South Wales. Forts at the river mouths ensured command of the littoral and the river valleys could be used to penetrate and outflank the Black Mountains and to force open the gateway to Brycheiniog by way of the upper Wye and the Usk. The importance of the Usk valley as an arterial route was emphasized by the foundation at its mouth of the legionary fortress at Caerleon (Isca Silurum), which for long remained the seat of the south-western command. Beyond the land of the Silures the area of Caermarthenshire and Pembrokeshire belonged to the Demetae, whose territory was encircled rather than penetrated by the strategic road-system, as if these people, probably hostile to the Silures, had welcomed rather than opposed the Romans. It cannot then have been difficult to absorb Mid-Wales between the Usk and Severn valleys, for much of the area is too wild for habitation. But north of the Severn the great wall of the Berwyns and the inner massif of Snowdonia screened and sheltered a second anti-Roman tribe, the Ordovices; and, while pushing garrisons hard against their boundaries, there Frontinus was compelled to stop. The strategical position in North Wales was not quite so easy to handle because effective control could be operated only from a point which looked north-eastwards towards the Brigantes as well as south-westwards towards Wales. Recent excavations at Chester have shown that the legionary fortress there was in process of erection towards the end of Frontinus' command, and that its use as a base for the conquest and organization of North Wales belongs to his successor, Iulius Agricola.

The occupation of Chester by legionaries was, however, preceded by an earlier military use of the site, which may well go back to the time of Suetonius Paulinus:

and the conquest of the Flintshire Deceangli cannot be
later than about this time, since their mines were producing ingots of lead in A.D. 74, by when the work of pacifica-
tion and organization must be regarded as completed. As
commander of the Twentieth Legion under the governor
Cerealis, Agricola must already have known this region
well and it is his previous knowledge of the area which
explains why, on his arrival as governor, late either in
A.D. 77 or in A.D. 78, he was ready to open a campaign
against the Ordovices at once. Their offence was grave:
they had almost annihilated a cavalry regiment stationed
on their borders; and the punishment was swift and grim.
Without hesitation Agricola marched a mixed punitive
force up into their territory – one thinks of the major line
of penetration through Cerrig-y-drudion and Bettws-y-
coed – wiped out almost the whole tribe and seized
Anglesey. After this it only remained to grip North Wales
by forts at the river mouths and by an inner line of penetration based upon the upper Dee valley and the work of
conquest was done. It was the first time in Britain that a
large mountainous region had been both conquered and
organized under military control, and the arrangement
provided the model for the treatment of the Brigantes and
other northern tribes.

There is no doubt that it was Agricola who rounded off
the consolidation of northern Britain, and that much of
his work took place upon the west coast, though his hand
is also traceable in County Durham and between Tyne
and Solway. The next two years saw campaigns carried
to the Tay and consolidation reaching the Forth-Clyde
isthmus, where a temporary line of forts and fortlets
barred out any counter move. The main task had been
the envelopment and penetration of the territory of the
Selgovae, who occupied the entire basin of the middle and

Figure 2

upper Tweed. The coastal tribe of the Votadini, stretching
from Northumberland to the Forth, also came into the
net, though without so strong a garrison and therefore
perhaps with more goodwill. Only when these areas were
settled could Agricola turn his attention westwards and
consider the problem of Galloway and its relation to
Ireland. Until air-photography and excavation recently
showed otherwise, it was thought that the Roman attitude towards Galloway was to shun it. Now it is evident
that not only Galloway but Ayrshire was penetrated by

Roman forces and dominated by permanent forts. This explains why Agricola should have considered with such vivid longing the conquest of Ireland and, conversely, why an Irish chieftain should have pinned his hopes upon Roman backing. Only those who have viewed the opposite coasts from either Larne or Portpatrick can realize how imminent the threat of conquest or how bright the opportunity must have seemed. On balance, however, the negative decision then taken was wise, when related to Roman resources in manpower, and none of the considerations arising on the spot outweighs that factor.

The year spent in consolidation behind the temporary frontier on the Forth-Clyde Isthmus was also used in giving consideration to the prospects beyond it. It was doubtless at this time that Agricola explored the west coast and its islands with the fleet, seconding the schoolmaster Demetrius of Tarsus to the party of exploration. Geographical inquiry was the prime purpose of the expedition, but its strategical aim must have been more special, namely to determine whether there was any way of circumventing or outflanking the Highland plateau. Previous reconnaissance, before the temporary line of the Forth-Clyde Isthmus was chosen, must have revealed that this was the cardinal problem which remained, and the action now taken by Agricola shows that he judged an outflanking move to be impossible. No such action as had taken place in South Wales was going to prove feasible in Scotland. The strategy now planned and skilfully applied during the next two years was to gain firm possession of Strathmore, the gateway to the north, to deny to northern attackers the use of it as a springboard, and then to provoke the northern tribes to a pitched battle of such a scale that its loss would cripple them for at least a generation or longer. That is the meaning of the

Figure 3. Fendoch, an Agricolan fort at the Highland gates

final operations of Agricola and their culmination in the great battle of Mons Graupius, which was a victory comparable with the later Culloden. The result was to leave the Romans in possession of all lowland Scotland with Highland resistance broken. On the strength of this notable achievement Agricola was recalled, after a longer governorship than the normal, and the Flavian forward movement was at an end.

If archaeology provided, as it has not yet done, a basis for an estimate of the number of auxiliary regiments employed in garrisoning the Claudio-Neronian frontiers in Britain, it would be possible to assess the extra strain placed upon the British garrison as the result of the Flavian forward movement. But if area counts for anything, the increase in territory policed by military troops as a result of the Flavian conquests was very great. The previous frontier, comprising the Fosse Way, its hinterland and its fringe, even if that fringe extended up to or beyond the Severn, hardly covers more than Wales demanded, while the northern frontier covered about two and a half times the area of Wales. But the increase was no isolated phenomenon: and the forward movement had gone ahead elsewhere on the frontiers of the Empire in response to similar needs of straightening out awkward salients and re-entrants or eliminating unreliable buffer States. The reverse side of the picture was the contribution in manpower which the newly-annexed areas could make, the quota of one area going to form the garrison of another. In this respect Britain had an important contribution to make to the grand scheme of Imperial defence, a living tribute which might be judged to make worth while the counter expenditure in garrisons.

But while thus lavish in its increase of the Roman auxiliary army the Flavian age made no corresponding increase in the legions. These formidable shock troops, at once the crack fighters and the skilled technicians of the Roman army, were the carefully balanced pieces on the chess-board of the Empire and their number was not even slightly increased without the weightiest reasons. The very conception of a balance of power between the different quarters of the Empire dictated, too, that there should be no mobile reserve of legions to disturb it. Consequently, when pressure fell heavily upon a given frontier, the sole means of substantial reinforcement was the stripping of others. When, therefore, pressure began to bear heavily upon the Danube frontier in the later eighties, it was felt politic to deprive Britain of a legion for service in Pannonia. The fact that this legion, on duty in the far north, was vital to the Agricolan scheme of British defences could be of no weight against danger on the frontier nearest to the heart of the Empire.

The legion chosen for Central Europe was II Adiutrix, largely raised in Pannonia, which had only been in Britain since A.D. 71 and had been stationed first at Lincoln and then at Chester. The northern legion, Agricola's most trusty unit, the Twentieth, was then withdrawn from Inchtuthil on the Tay to Chester, where it remained for centuries. The move was inevitable, for the Chester position had to be filled whatever happened further north. Until now the northern permanent defences had consisted of a line of forts blocking the Highland passes, linked to a trunk road passing north from the Forth. At least one of these, at Fendoch in Glenalmond, was abandoned. But the grip upon Strathearn held firm and the organization of defence in the Lowlands was now pivoted upon Newstead, where a great and massive reconstruction of the fort took place and legionaries and auxiliaries were brigaded together. There is no sign of the

Figure 4. Caerleon, a Trajanic legionary fortress

slackening of this grip until about A.D. 100, when all the forts north of the Cheviot and perhaps north of the Tyne-Solway gap were evacuated. But whether this contraction of commitments was due to increasing enemy pressure or to a deliberate attempt to reduce the British garrison still further is not apparent. All that can be said is that it coincided with a firm consolidation of legionary fortresses and forts further south. The process seems to have begun at Caerleon in A.D. 99 and to have spread thence to auxiliary forts throughout Wales. It is discernible at Chester after A.D. 102 and at York in A.D. 108–9: but it is not so certain how far it extended to the forts of the north, for many reconstructions in stone which were once thought to fit the consolidation of Trajan now prove to be linked with activity at the end of the reign of Antoninus Pius. At Corbridge, for example, one of the biggest and most important forts in the north, there is no pre-Antonine reconstruction of the site in stone.

The consolidation of the military area in Britain under Trajan is a corollary of his intense contemporary activity in Dacia, where British auxiliary regiments played a gallant part, and of his later campaigns in the Orient. But the silence which ensued is due to lack of sources and must not be mistaken for proved tranquillity. Certain it is that immediately after Trajan's death in A.D. 117 trouble came which involved heavy Roman casualties and which Fronto, writing two generations later, remembered as especially notable. This is to be connected with the fact that by A.D. 122 the Ninth Legion was replaced at York by the Sixth and disappeared from the army lists thereafter. That the Legion was cashiered there is no doubt and it seems evident that this fate, at the hands of the disciplinarian Hadrian, followed an ignominious defeat. But the unit was not annihilated. Some of its officers at least survived and nothing whatever is reported of the circumstances or place of the trouble. The steps which Hadrian took to repair the damage suggest, however, that the seat of disturbance lay in south-western Scotland.

This great consolidator of the Empire took in Britain, as elsewhere, an engineer's view of the problem. The work of Augustus, who chose natural barriers for the Imperial frontiers, was to be supplemented by artificial

barriers where required, and of these Hadrian's Wall in
Britain, between Tyne and Solway, was at once the
shortest and the most impressive in scale and in siting.
Beginning, as first planned, at Pons Aelius (Newcastle
upon Tyne) and choosing the shortest route from sea to
sea south of the Cheviot, it grips the northern rim of the
Tyne and Irthing valleys and terminates on the southern
shore of the Solway beyond its lowest ford. The whole
barrier was at first seventy-six Roman miles long. The
eastern forty-five miles were closed by a Wall of stone,
ten Roman feet wide and some sixteen high to rampart
walk, the western thirty-one by a rampart of turf, twenty
Roman feet wide at the base and some twelve feet high.
These barriers were fronted, wherever needed, by a
great ditch and were patrolled from attached fortlets, or
milecastles, placed at every Roman mile, with two turrets
between them. These parts of the defences were designed
to prevent infiltration. The second problem was the
defence against attacks. For this purpose each milecastle
was provided with a wide sally-port, through any of
which the fighting garrisons stationed behind the Wall
might issue to encircle attackers and drive them against
the barrier, like hunters using a corral. Thus employed,
Roman disciplined tactics and superior equipment could
be made to tell. But such a tactical disposition could be
put into action much better if the fighting garrison was
placed upon the Wall itself and this was the sense of an
important change of plan, carried out while the work was
still under construction. The Wall was supplied in stages
with its sixteen well-known forts, covering all main lines
of approach, and was itself extended eastwards from
Newcastle to Wallsend, increasing its length to eighty
Roman miles. Once this change took place the entire
work could be marked off from its wild hinterland by a

continuous cleared strip or *limes*, known as the Vallum, bordered by mounds and made into a formidable obstacle by a deep flat-bottomed ditch running along its axis. All that then remained was to replace the turf rampart by a rampart of stone. This substitution had already begun during the fort-building, when the stone wall from North Tyne to a point five miles west of the Irthing had been erected at a thickness reduced to eight Roman feet and the vast building programme ended in a final extension of the work in stone throughout Cumberland. Two subsidiary provisions remain to be mentioned. The west flank of the system was protected for over thirty miles by equipping the Cumberland shore with milefortlets and towers, organized like the milecastles and turrets of the Wall but unconnected by a barrier. Secondly, the Cumbrian approaches, including the Solway fords, were screened by outpost-forts as Bewcastle, Netherby, and Birrens. These provisions appear to belong to the original scheme.

The great work was thus at length finished. Construction began in A.D. 122 or 123: the work on the forts was completed not very long after A.D. 128. It seems certain that the first designers did not intend the task to have taken so long: certain also that the additions to the scheme imply a mounting intensity of attack upon the barrier and a need to keep unwanted folk on the south away from the military zone. But the changes can also be viewed as an adaptation of what was already there to local circumstances which the original designers had not appreciated accurately.

x The unforeseen degree of pressure which the Wall had to withstand attests the irritation which this application of the new type of closed frontier caused among the excluded tribesmen. On the Roman side the scheme undoubtedly resulted in economy of manpower. Wales seems to have been largely denuded of troops to supply the Wall-garrison, and in the hinterland of the Wall there was a reorganization of garrisons. But the external pressure and internal economy were soon considered together in another fashion. Pressure could be reduced if Lowland Scotland were reoccupied: manpower expenditure would not be increased if the Pennines could be denuded of troops after the fashion of Wales. Further, the reservoir of fighting men now potentially, and perhaps actually, so vexatious to defenders of the Wall could be drained away and drafted for service in another province with great advantage to the Imperial budget of manpower.

Some such thoughts as these seem to have influenced the next phase of Imperial policy in Britain, which was a swing from the Hadrianic recession to a forward movement. The new advance put into practice few novel conceptions. Agricola's forts were for the most part reoccupied, but the system was stiffened by a new frontier in the Hadrianic manner, with modifications due to experience. The differences are of some interest. There was no rearward Vallum; milecastles and turrets were eliminated; a much larger ditch was dug in front of the Wall, which is itself turf-built but equally steep and difficult to scale at back and front. The forts are smaller and more closely spaced, so that smaller garrisons might act more quickly and in closer concert in rounding-up the enemy against the barrier and its great ditch. Tactically considered, the Antonine Wall was in fact less an imitation of the great work which it superseded than a skilfully devised improvement upon it. Strategically, however, it is more open to criticism. Its flanks are weak, and the weakness is emphasized by the precautions taken to avoid it. All Fife had to be encircled in order to prevent its use

Figure 5

HADRIAN'S WALL AND ITS OUTPOSTS

as a spring-board for an attack on the east. The western precautions are less certain, but they include arrangements for patrolling the south bank of the Clyde estuary, where this flank is weakest; and a fortified approach-road through the pass of Darvel implies an occupation of the Ayrshire coast, whence the distance to free Kintyre seems a stone's throw on a fine day.

The conscious imitation of Agricola's tactics is reflected in a telling phrase borrowed from his biography to describe the work. 'The barbarians were moved up', as it were into another island. The phrase has been connected, probably wrongly, with another consequence of the new extension of the province, namely, the appearance in the Neckar zone of the German frontier of new irregular detachments of Brittones. These are best explained as levies exacted from conquered tribes who had surrendered unconditionally. They were established in the German frontier area. With them, to settle them in, went officials drawn from the provincial garrison and it was no doubt such overseers who introduced to the German frontier fashions in stonework recognizably derived from the British command. A hint of the denuded land, its populace depleted but not exterminated, is afforded by the disposition of the garrison of the hinterland. It lay now in widely spaced forts, linked by roads studded with small posts, intended both to protect convoys and to check unauthorized movement. And it is noteworthy that the system is most evident in south-west Scotland, where anti-Roman aggression had been heaviest. The wide-spacing of the main garrison indicates a depleted and disarmed populace: the frequent posts denote rigorous and watchful control. The arrangement is not so unlike the Highland dispositions of General Wade after the conquest of 1745.

FIRTH OF FORTH

Carriden
Kinneil
Inveravon
Mumrills
Camelon
Falkirk
Rough Castle
Seabegs
Castlecary
Westerwood
Croy Hill
Bar Hill
Auchendavy
Lurgie
Kirkintilloch
Cadder
Balmuildy
Yorkhill
New Kilpatrick
Castle Hill
Duntocher
Old Kilpatrick
Bishopton
Lurg Moor

Avon
Carron
Kelvin
Blane
Loch Lomond

CLYDE

Bothwellhaugh

FIRTH OF CLYDE

THE ANTONINE WALL

5   0   5   10 Miles

Figure 6

The barrier of Hadrian's Wall was for the time being thrown open freely. The Wall itself ceased to be patrolled; only its forts were held, often by less mobile garrisons; the doors and the milecastle gateways were dismantled; the Vallum was furnished with frequent unimpeded crossings. Among the Brigantes forts were freely scrapped, as if with the advancement of the frontier a new age of peace had begun. But it was not long before the situation changed.

The revolt of A.D. 155–8 is marked partly by reconstructions and partly by records of troop movements. An important fort was rebuilt at Birrens and a new fort was planted on a deserted Flavian site at Brough (Derbyshire). Birrens lies forward from the west end of the Tyne-Solway gap; Brough, succeeded by the modern Castleton, is the natural centre of the Peak District, exploited for its rich supplies of lead. The two places lie too far apart to assume without further proof that the land between them was aflame with revolt. But the troop movements begin to fill in the picture; reinforcements for all three British legions were landed in the Tyne, direct from the German provinces, and at Corbridge a dedication by an officer of the Sixth Legion attests casualties for which revenge was exacted. The concentration of activity on the Tyne is surely significant of a determination to hold firmly the southern isthmus as a base for operations further north and of a hesitation to operate freely until reinforcements had arrived. What seems certain is the temporary loss of territory to north of Hadrian's Wall. What is more doubtful is the state of affairs further south: but some light is shed upon this by the further rebuilding, under the governor Calpurnius Agricola. He was responsible for a complete rebuilding at Corbridge and Chesterholm, and for important work at Ribchester and Hardknott on the west coast, probably amounting to total reconstruction. A new fort also occurs at Melandra near Glossop, neighbour to Brough. This would suggest that in the wilder parts of Brigantia, amid the forests and fells of Cumberland and north Lancashire, there had been sufficient unrest to call for re-occupation and that this had pinned down the army of Britain upon the Tyne-Solway isthmus until reinforcements arrived. A Roman would have said that they 'held a wolf by the ears', a stalemate only to be relieved by help from outside.

The consequence of this situation was a temporary evacuation of the Scottish Wall and the Lowland forts, and, when re-occupation came, a simultaneous holding of Hadrian's Wall as well. Much shuffling of garrisons was needed to effect this, and in the zone beyond the Forth-Clyde isthmus forts were reduced in size, while traces of similar measures to save manpower are discernible in lesser degree in the land behind it. These measures too are almost certainly to be ascribed to Calpurnius Agricola, but the direct proof afforded by inscriptions is lacking. But at all excavated sites north of Hadrian's Wall evidence for a reconstruction of about this time has been found: and it is reasonable to link it with the better documented series of reconstructions, which cannot in any case have been isolated. One of the new measures deserves special note. Newstead, the great fort which was the pivot of activity in the Lowlands, received a larger cavalry garrison than ever before, an *ala* one thousand strong. These costly and valuable regiments, almost rarer than the legions, were habitually placed upon frontiers where attacks in force, which called for a rapid and decisive repulse, might be made on a fairly wide front. The change suggests, firstly, that the northern territory was yielding enough to make its retention desirable and, secondly, that thrusts of some strength had been probing for weak spots in its defences.

The next record of disturbance in the north, in the opening years of the Emperor Commodus, mentions just such a thrust and its authors, the barbarians beyond the Wall. They broke through and did serious damage, killing a legate and his men. There is no disturbance of the period on Hadrian's Wall and the Antonine Wall must be meant. The disaster was also followed by a sharp punitive campaign. Whether the damage included a devastation of the whole Scottish Wall is a point upon which no certainty has yet been reached. Excavation has produced no decisive material for dating its final period of occupation and current opinion is divided between a reconstruction now, followed by a short final occupation, or a destruction in or shortly before A.D. 196 and a short occupation under Severus. Either view is possible, though the second places more strain upon the lack of evidence.

Whatever actually happened, an event occurred at the close of the century which must unquestionably coincide with a break in the occupation of the northern frontier. In A.D. 193, when Commodus had been assassinated and the line of Imperial succession was broken, Septimius Severus, governor of Moesia, used his army to make himself Emperor. Others were ready to do the same. Pescennius Niger, governor of Syria, and Clodius Albinus, governor of Britain, were both rival claimants and Severus, playing one off against the other, recognized Albinus as Caesar, or heir-apparent, in order to gain time. But Albinus was in fact preparing for a civil war with the support of the army of Britain, and when Severus broke off relations in A.D. 196 Albinus was ready to transfer much of his army to the Continent, leaving the northern defences empty or weakened to breaking point behind him. There was no turning back and the army felt it; in two battles, the second decisive, the army of Britain, using with deadly effect its leaden missiles, almost won the day. When it was beaten, the province went to the victor.

It was a wasted military heritage into which Severus entered. On the news of the defeat of Albinus, the northern tribes had broken in, plundering and burning. Almost every excavated fort between York and the north shows traces of destruction at this time, and the walls of York itself had to be rebuilt from their foundations. But Chester appears to have stood unscathed, though Wroxeter may have now been raided and partly destroyed. If so, it is the only British tribal capital that shows signs of destruction at the time, as if Severus had taken very prompt measures to save the civil area of the province. Strong military action was out of the question. The northern raiders were bought off and time was thus gained for the reconstruction of the base of York and of the wasted forts, hardly less than thirty in number from Hadrian's Wall southwards. As a whole the work took time. The forts of Yorkshire and Stainmore were put in hand within a year: but work was still in progress in the rest of the area, and in Yorkshire too, almost a decade later, under the governor of A.D. 205–8. By that date, however, Hadrian's Wall was rebuilt, together with the outpost forts beyond it, now extended to cover Northumberland as well as the western approaches to the Wall. Further, the governor Alfenus Senecio was operating beyond and winning victories in A.D. 206. However, his report summing up the situation at this time was realistic enough. 'The need was either more troops to reinforce the frontier area, or an Imperial expedition.' In terms of earlier events and previous treatment of the problem the

meaning of this report is unmistakable. The aggressors
were the Maeatae of Strathmore and Strathearn, who
later became the southern part of the Pictish nation. In
the past they had been held in check by occupying at
least the southern portion of their territory, and the need
to control them and to trammel their movement had
brought the Romans into the lower Tay basin. Unless
that were to be done again, in the manner of the Anto-
nines, or unless a great expedition could be mounted
against the northern tribes, in the manner of the Flavians,
the settled conditions so seriously disrupted in A.D. 197
would not return. Severus chose the second alternative,
partly in order to get his two sons away from the capital,
much more in order to give to both the experience in
organization that they required and to prepare them for
joint rule in due course. Thus, on the coins of Caracalla,
who had been joint Augustus since the defeat of Albinus,
preparations for the British expedition are so prominently
heralded by A.D. 207 as to have raised the question
whether Caracalla was not already in the province. It
was, however, in A.D. 208 that Severus, his Empress and
Geta arrived in Britain, and Severus began with Caracalla the year of preparation for a northern campaign
which at once intimidated the tribes concerned into su-
ing for peace. When the year was over the attack was
delivered not against the Maeatae but against the
Caledonians. This explains why the base for the expedition was fixed upon the Firth of Forth and supplied by
sea, while much preparation of roads was undertaken in
marshy country, a description suitable to Angus and the
Mearns or to Fife but hardly to the long-established land-
route between Forth and Tay, which would require no
more than refurbishing. The effects of the expedition
were rapid and thorough. The Caledonians were beaten

into unconditional surrender, with laying down of arms and contribution of levies. It is worth while to emphasize that the ceremony of surrender took place in Caledonia and that this was more than any other Roman conqueror ever achieved. The next winter, however, the Maeatae flared into revolt, and had themselves to be punished by a further campaign, while a winter later both groups broke into revolt again, and were only saved from a war of extermination by the death of Severus in February, A.D. 211. One further campaign followed, suppressed by historians hostile to Caracalla but attested by the coins, and peace-terms were then laid down, while Caracalla withdrew all Roman garrisons to the line of Hadrian's Wall and its forward zone. The undertaking which the Maeatae and Caledonians had broken was not to unite in common action. This at least must have been insisted upon, while, if the campaign was originally undertaken to protect the lands north of Hadrian's Wall, a coherent picture of the new arrangement begins to emerge. The northern tribes, soon to be known as Picts, divided into two groups, were to abstain from raiding their Brythonic neighbours south of the Forth. The Brythonic tribes, until recently enveloped within the Empire, were still to be protected by Roman arms but left without garrisons, much as the Frisii or the Hermunduri were treated on the Rhine or Danube. For the better control of their territory, the new outpost-forts of Hadrian's Wall were equipped with large and semi-mobile garrisons, and became also the headquarters for irregular units of *exploratores* or frontier patrol-men. The occupied zone of the new model frontier thus extended not merely to the Cheviot, but its patrols ranged still further afield, to Lothian, Upper Clydesdale, or Galloway. This implies a measure of regulated control of the Lowland tribes which is echoed in the list of their authorized meeting-places or *loca*, recently recognized to exist in the geographical document known as the Ravenna Cosmography. It is indicated also in the character of the new native settlements, devoid of formidable defences and frequently lacking any defences at all. Here may be recognized the controlling hand of Rome which guaranteed peace and licensed only barriers against wild beasts and chance marauders. Very similar arrangements are discernible in Wales, where the native fortifications of the period are of the same type, civil defences rather than military works.

The dispositions of Caracalla thus deserve more credit than they have often received. They guaranteed peace in northern Britain for longer than the action of any other Roman general ever enforced it; and they seem to have achieved this despite the serious worsening of political and economic conditions that afflicted the Empire during the frequent collapses of central authority in the middle and later years of the third century A.D. As the century drew to a close the troubles besetting Britain were of a new kind, namely, sea-raids by Pictish and Saxon pirates.

A make-shift measure against Saxon raiders can be recognized at Richborough, where, in the last quarter of the third century A.D., the lofty triumphal monument commemorating the conquest of the island was girt by ditches and converted into a look-out post. The system seems to have been related to warning the fleet of approaching hostile craft, with a view to their interception. Interception was certainly the basic tactical idea, whether the pirates were caught on the way in or the way out, for these are the operations described in the career of Carausius, the admiral of the *classis Britannica*. It was an accusation that he waited too often for the return journey of the pirates, and shared their booty with them, that led to his act of usurpation. Rather than risk a trial, Carausius seized Britain and the Low Countries and had himself proclaimed Augustus. His island Empire, recognized for a while by central authority, lasted for six years, when he was assassinated by his chief finance officer, Allectus, who was not overcome for another three. During the nine years (A.D. 287–96) Carausius and Allectus began the system of coastal defences known as the Saxon Shore. These works, built partly in the old style, based upon earthworks, and partly to the new pattern, based upon elaborate town defences, ran from the Norfolk coast to the Isle of Wight. Their function was to house mixed garrisons of soldiers and sailors, for intercepting raiders both by land and sea; and they could be used in combination as bases for sea-patrols. Nor were such foundations confined to the south-east coast of the island. On the west coast they are, indeed, much less well known: but examples occur at Cardiff and at Lancaster and these cannot have stood alone. It is probable, however, that the western examples, and some of the Saxon Shore forts too, belong to the restoration of Constantius I, who re-united the island to the Empire in A.D. 296. His victory, like that of Severus, cost him the northern frontier, which Allectus had stripped of troops and which was invaded and wasted when he was defeated. This time the damage was worse, for it included Chester as well as York, as if the Scotti of Northern Ireland were now among the sea-raiders by whom the island was threatened. But with Roman constancy and pertinacity the damage was repaired and in good fashion. York, indeed, rose statelier than ever before, with a fortress whose river-front was a grandiose version of the newest style in military architecture: while the land approaches to the Vale of York were dominated by new forts of great size holding mounted garrisons big enough to hunt down and overwhelm even the largest raiding bands. The new prosperity of the area, of which more will be said in a later chapter (p. 109), is an indication of the success of these vigorous measures.

The sea-patrols of the period deserve special mention, since they gained a place in classical literature. Vegetius, who dedicated his work to Valentinian I (A.D. 364–75), describes the contemporary scout-ships. They were fast, light craft, their hulls and rigging painted sea-green and their crew of twenty rowers clad in sea-green clothing. They were named *Pictae*, presumably because they resembled Pictish curraghs (*curucae*), and their task was not to engage enemy ships but to report their movements to the Roman fleet.

The most eloquent testimony to the general success of these measures was the reaction which in due time they prompted. After some sixty years of frustration the barbarians, among whom concerted action was so rare as to be outside Roman reckoning, resorted to a great joint attack. In A.D. 367 the Saxons, Picts, and Scots made a synchronized assault upon the province, killing the Count of the Saxon Shore, who was head of coastal defence, and immobilizing the Duke of the Britains, who was commander-in-chief of inland forces. The Wall and the forts of the north again fell, and it is recorded that the cause of this item in the chapter of disaster was the treachery of the frontier scouts, who were bought over by promises of a share in the loot. There were also many cases of desertion.

When the storm was over and Count Theodosius, bringing numerous new troops with him, had restored order, it was a different frontier world that arose in the north. Until now the Wall had been garrisoned by troops organized in regular regiments, however territorialized such units may have become through local recruiting or through hereditary obligations to army service. The Wall forts had attracted substantial extra-mural civil settlements, especially where, as at House-steads (Borcovicium), there was an established market for trade beyond the frontier. Now that those settlements had perished amid fire and slaughter they were not renewed. The new garrisons, with their women and children, lived exclusively within the forts, crudely recon-structed by provincial labour. The forts thus became little fortified townships, more like a medieval Conway, Beaumaris, or Flint than a Roman *castellum*, and in medieval fashion the garrisons received the surrounding land to cultivate in return for their services. How such organization, or lack of it, played havoc with the internal disposition of buildings still arranged on traditional lines is revealed at not a few forts, where granaries became dwellings and headquarters buildings became half store-houses and half living-quarters. A centurion of the old order would have blenched at the sight.

Such garrisons as these, farmer-soldiers no longer at the old pitch of readiness, could not be given the task of patrolling the outlands, where the old patrol-system had in any case broken down. To meet the new situation, the tribes of the outlands, who had grown in political experi-ence under Roman tutelage, were given increased inde-pendence, and converted from protectorates into *foeder-ati* or treaty states. The two groups were the Damnonii of Strathclyde and the Votadini of Lothian and North-umberland, the later Bernicia, whose native dynasties have authentic pedigrees going back to this period and also names and titles which suggest Roman influence and Roman suzerainty. This may be regarded as the good fruit yielded by the policy of Caracalla, which first converted the south of Scotland into protectorates that were in reality buffer states.

Elsewhere than in the furthest north new measures continued to be taken. The best known example is on the Yorkshire coast, which was equipped with up-to-date fortlets containing great towers to espy and to signal the approach of sea-raiders. These were almost certainly intended to set naval operations in train for interception, for they lie in part on the fringe of desolate country, devoid of routes to the interior and conspicuously bad in lateral roadways and are comprehensible only as transmitting intelligence coastwise Some forts, again, were reoccupied, as, for example, Caernarvon in North Wales, adjacent to copper deposits of considerable value. There is every indication that a firm hold was kept upon the nerve-centre of the north at York and upon the large inland forts connected therewith, such as Malton and Piercebridge. These and the naval ports were the bases from which the long arm of Rome could still strike. After A.D. 367 a naval repair-depot was still operating in the Bristol Channel; and it must be significant that the very last offensive measures in Britain, ascribed by a Roman writer to Stilicho, were naval raids following the usurpation of Magnus Maximus of A.D. 383–8. Whether these actually took place or not, the fruits of comparable action on the part of the Roman government may be clearly recognized in the regiments of Scotti and Atecotti forming part of the Continental army of the Emperor Honorius. These represent levies from overseas outside the British province, either exacted after offensive action or bought by Roman gold, but in any case relieving pressure upon the coasts of Britain. The Scotti came from Northern Ireland and the Atecotti probably from the western littoral of Scotland.

If the final stages of defence and the new devolution of responsibility for it in the north can thus be traced with some approach to the truth, the position in other parts of the island is less sure. But it is important for an understanding of the latest phase of Romano-British military activity on the East Coast that East Anglia and the East Riding adjacent to York are filled both with late-Roman pottery in Saxon taste and with some of the earliest Saxon cemeteries in Britain, comparable with those of the late fourth and early fifth century A.D. on the Continent. It suggests very strongly that Honorius, if not his predecessors, had adopted for Britain the policy of settling folk of the outlands, in this case Saxons, in the border territories of the Empire which they had once come to rob, giving them lands in exchange for military service. The precise bearing of this upon Saxon settlement in Britain cannot as yet be documented or traced. But it at least places the tradition of Hengist and Horsa in a continuity, making the event less isolated and more comprehensible. Vortigern's action can be seen as forming part of the pattern of devolution rather than as a new and untried remedy by a desperate and inexperienced native prince.

CHAPTER TWO

TOWNS AND URBAN CENTRES

THE military history of Roman Britain derives not a little of its interest from the variety and ingenuity of its pattern, which stamps it as a lively and vigorous reaction to Imperial problems, now external and now internal. But the basic assumption behind all such action is that there was a province worth protection, a land which paid dividends in either taxation, or troops, or raw materials; these yields were sufficient, singly or in combination, to justify an occupation on grounds of expense, quite apart from the over-riding strategical considerations which originally and continually made the occupation desirable. An occupation, furthermore, in conferring peace and order, brought about the conditions in which population and productivity might be substantially increased. The tribute yield of the Three Gauls was doubled in fifty years, and while the expansion cannot have continued at so prodigious a rate, it remains a valuable indication of what might happen in the first tide of peace and prosperity among people who did not welcome the new order with unanimity.

The instrument of civilization used by Rome in achieving such results was the town and the many-sided attainments of amenity and social grace which successful civic organization involves. No false modesty or feeling for others inhibited the Roman belief in their own hybrid civilization, though they enjoyed analysing its shams and pretences with the scorn of a quick-witted and confident race. The normal method of introducing the instrument in Celtic lands, where the most important political unit was the council of jealous tribal notables, was through the aristocratic families. These were encouraged to adopt Roman ways and to give their sons a Roman education, absorbing these things as the inward stamp of a new civilization whose outward habits and equipment possessed the magnetism of novelty and the prestige of success. Once this movement got under way the rest would follow. Tribal revenues, private generosity, and family pride or emulation could be devoted to creating an urban centre for tribal government, tribal festivals, and tribal markets, which had meanwhile been left undisturbed by the Roman provincial administration as far as was compatible with its needs. At this stage the Roman government lent a hand. The development was not permitted until the financial soundness of the proposal had been examined and approved. Then a surveyor or architect might be lent and a new town or local government centre would begin to rise, with its lands duly apportioned and its streets laid off in Roman manner.

But to suppose that this happened in the first years of development of the province is to go too fast. The earliest phase of Romano-British tribal capitals is much more modest and begins with traders gathered at the tribal centre, in simple timber shacks and workshops. Such agglomerations have been noted under Claudius at Verulamium (St Albans), Isca Dumnoniorum (Exeter), and Ratae Coritanorum (Leicester), the first in the form of ribbon development along a Roman road. This is a natural growth, matched at early Gallic capitals such as Bibracte (Mont Beuvray). Meanwhile, those who might further such matters had to learn what a Roman town was like. In a new overseas province this was difficult, and it was not until seven years after the invasion that the

governor Ostorius Scapula set about founding and building such a place on the site of the capital of Cunobelinus
at Camulodunum (Colchester). The primary object of
the foundation was to provide a chartered town or *colonia*
for veteran legionaries, who would receive a house-plot
in the town and an amount of cultivable land outside it
appropriate to their rank. But in such foundations local
inhabitants might also share, within defined limits, and
it is clear that the Trinovantes had a place at Camulodunum. Towns of the kind, with their sewered streets in
ordered rectangular plan, imposing public buildings,
comfortable private houses, and a good town-wall were
not erected quickly. Twenty or twenty-five years might
well elapse from start to finish, and the order of building
the several elements varied. At Camulodunum after
eleven years a senate-house, theatre, and private dwellings existed, but work on the town defences had not yet
begun. Above all, much time had been spent upon erecting the Temple of Claudius which was to be the centre of
Emperor-worship for the whole province. Roman historians remarked, looking back upon these events, how
amenities had come first: and this is comprehensible,
when the political and cultural education of the native
aristocracy was the first and fundamental condition of
civilizing the province as a whole.

How the cult of the Emperor could take its place in the
scheme needs explanation. In Rome and among Roman
citizens the world over, the living Emperor was the first
citizen, deriving his power and authority from the
Senate; only after death was an Emperor of good repute
deified. But among the lower orders of citizens, the over-
whelming power and prestige of the Emperor led to his
receiving divine honours while alive, and in higher circles
also the same reaction was frequent enough. To this view,

in much more extravagant form, the eastern half of the Empire, long used to the idea of divine kingship, needed no conversion. In the west, where the Emperor had sole charge of almost every province beyond the Alps, the idea was employed politically. The tribes of free Gaul had been wont to meet in a sacred annual convention to discuss common interests and to perform common rites. When Druidism was forbidden by Rome, on the ground of its abhorrent human sacrifices, the annual tribal meeting was reconstituted at the new provincial capital under the auspices of Rome and Augustus. The tribes elected from among themselves a priest and priestess to hold office for a year, maintaining the calendared ritual and presiding over the great annual festival of games and contests in literature and music. But the new proceedings were conducted in Latin, for the honour and welfare of the Roman state, and the festival thus became a focus of loyalty and Romanization. The Claudian plan was to establish a similar institution for Britain, centred at Camulodunum. For several reasons the venture was not a success. It was not founded upon tradition, for the British tribes held no common meeting; it was probably too sharp a transition; it was certainly too costly a burden, because it fell too often upon too few tribes. Finally, it chose for its object of devotion not Rome and the Emperor, a conception sufficiently august to survive political mischances, but Claudius himself, whose court and administration were notorious no less for their corruption than for his failure to perceive it. This explains why, in certain quarters, the venture bred discontent and disillusionment rather than comprehension and enthusiasm. The revolt of A.D. 61, in which the new *colonia* perished in flames and its inhabitants in massacre or torture, was in part fed upon local revulsion towards a cult

which had made a bad psychological start and was prov-
ing too heavy an economic burden.

British communities had thus to find their own way
towards a civilization which attracted them at first by its
convenience rather than by its subjective qualities. How
the start was made in many has already been indicated.
But there is one town which introduces another political
gradation, namely, the capital of a kingdom which was
left to itself as an independent unit within the province
and even granted sovereignty over other tribes. This was
the realm of Cogidumnus, known as Regnum, and its
folk as the Regnenses. The territory lay in a significant
position, on the left flank of the first Roman advance upon
the Thames, and on the right flank of their second advance, against the Belgae of Wiltshire and the Durotriges
of Dorset. Further, the study of pre-Claudian native
coins in Britain seems to show clearly enough that the
area was threatened by both the groups whom the
Romans were attacking and that it had formerly belonged
to the pro-Roman Verica. Whether Cogidumnus, its
ruler under Claudius, was a descendant of Verica is quite
unknown and it is perhaps suggestive that he makes no
claim to be so. But it is certain that he became a Roman
client-king on the initial organization of the province and
it may well be that his territory was the springboard for
Legate Vespasian's attack upon the west. His capital,
Noviomagus (Chichester), has yielded two remarkable
inscriptions, one lost, the other preserved, which illustrate the duties of a client-king. The lost piece was a
dedication in honour of the Emperor Nero, dated to
either A.D. 58 or 60. The text is an elaborate statement of
his Imperial ancestry and expressed with punctilious
accuracy the reverence which a subject king was expected
to have for his lord the Emperor. The second stone, which

is not dated, is a dedication of a temple to Neptune and Minerva by a gild of iron-workers on the authority of Cogidumnus, who is described as *Tiberius Claudius Cogidumnus, rex et legatus Augusti in Britannia*. This unique title implies that Cogidumnus had been endowed not only with Roman citizenship but with legatine authority within the province equivalent to that of a legionary legate, who had the insignia of a praetor, the second grade of senatorial magistrates. At the other side of the Roman world King Herod Agrippa had received comparable insignia, but not the legatine authority; and it is this conferment of Roman rank which attests in remarkable fashion the confidence felt in Cogidumnus by the Imperial Government, which had placed more than one other tribe under his rule. The rest of the inscription indicates his efforts to foster, as became a client-king, the Romanization of his realm. This is demonstrated by the dedication to Roman deities, first the god of the sea, over which the Wealden iron was brought to Chichester, and then the goddess of the craft which fashioned it, by the iron-workers' gild organized in Roman style: and, above all, by the wording of the text in solemn Roman legal diction. Structural remains of the period are not yet known at this native prince's capital. But the inscriptions are for Britain a rare and valuable documentation of the activities of its principal philo-Roman prince. They indicate how much might be done upon the initiative of a single potentate.

By the last quarter of the century ambitions were growing larger and the credit for their development is given by Tacitus to Agricola, though it seems clear that this intelligent governor was not in fact the first to take advantage of the current tendency. It is to this period that the street systems of Isca Dumnoniorum (Exeter), Calleva

Atrebatum (Silchester), and Corinium Dobunnorum
(Cirencester) belong. Camulodunum (Colchester) and
Verulamium (St Albans) were rising anew out of the
ashes of the Boudiccan revolt. The inhabitants of the old
hill-fort capital of the Durotriges moved down into the
plain and on to the Roman trunk road at Durnonovaria
(Dorchester), thereafter one of the two capitals of the
tribe. Two new *coloniae* for veterans were also founded,
at Lindum (Lincoln) and at Glevum (Gloucester), while
at Aquae Sulis (Bath) the curative hot springs appear to
have received their first stone buildings, precursors of an
establishment bigger than any of its kind in the Roman
West. Plainly the first reactions were over; enthusiasms
were perhaps moderated, antipathies certainly calmed,
and with the economic development of the province new
markets and new needs were bringing fresh opportunities
to capital and a return to investment. The native aristocracy was in the best position to profit by the settled peace
and could now afford to consider the development of
public amenities.

On the official governmental side it is instructive to
compare the new *coloniae* of Lindum (Lincoln) and
Glevum (Gloucester) with the new Camulodunum. The
latter covered within its walls 108 acres and there is good
evidence that the chess-board street-plan within them was
laid out in Nero's later years. The temple of Claudius, of
which the great vaulted platform was fireproof and
indestructible, occupied its old position. The town round
about it was as big as Roman Cologne, the *colonia
Agrippinensis* which was intended not only for Roman
veterans but for native inhabitants as well. Lindum and
Glevum, on the other hand, each covered just over forty
acres, and are so alike that the same public works contractors might have built them. Lincoln was for veterans

of the Ninth Legion, Gloucester for those of the Second
Augusta. It is possible that Camulodunum, the *colonia
Victricensis*, was for veterans from the two legions called
Victrix, the Fourteenth and Twentieth, and this might
account for its double size. But there is still room for other
classes of inhabitant, and nothing is known of the size
of the veteran drafts. Lincoln and Gloucester, on the
other hand, compare closely with such foundations as the
African Thamugadi (Timgad), a small and purely
Roman unit whose lands were carved out of native territory and whose town-plan and buildings were ostenta-
tiously and deliberately Roman in all their features.
Their *territoria*, it should be noted, are in the lands of
allied tribes, the Coritani of Lincolnshire and Leicester
and the Dobunni of the Cotswolds. But they are terrain
of a character which would be useless until Roman enterprise drained and developed it. Their loss might thus
ultimately be envied but could not be immediately
regarded as a hardship: and this suggests that the Romans
had duly noted the feelings aroused by harsh expropria-
tions at Camulodunum.

Different from any of the towns hitherto considered was
Londinium (London). Nature here contained the tidal
Thames within hard gravel banks and made possible the
construction of a bridge, where land traffic and sea
traffic for the whole island met. The roads radiated from
the bridge head, the sea lanes converged upon it from
the Rhine, the Gallic coastal ports, and the North Sea or
by the Channel route from Bordeaux, Spain, and the
Mediterranean. No question of status could prevent
Londinium from becoming the natural centre for
British trade and administration once the Roman engineer had picked it. If the first intention was to govern the
province from Camulodunum, it is clear that within a

generation the financial administration was using Londinium as its headquarters; while in the fourth century
A.D. it was not only the seat of the provincial treasury but
the residence of the civil governor who presided over the
four divisions into which the province was then broken.
In A.D. 100, if not before, the town was garrisoned like a
provincial capital, and it seems certain that, whatever
Camulodunum had been, the supremacy had by then
passed to Londinium. It is thus no accident that London
should furnish mercantile documents on wooden tablets,
a large city-hall for judicial and commercial business,
fine imported artistic works in bronze and marble, and
evidence of general Romanization upon a scale matched
in no other town in Roman Britain. It grew steadily, and
when its walls were built, in the second century A.D., they
enclosed an area of 325 acres, larger than most Roman
cities north of the Alps. As a trading centre the place was
already well known when it was reduced to ashes during
the rebellion of A.D. 61. During the following generation
it was growing rapidly, like a boom town, and was
ravaged by a great fire, dated to the twenties of the
second century A.D., only to emerge phoenix-like from its
ashes. Many of its buildings were no doubt half-timbered
and the fire-fighting appliances of the Roman world were
helpless against major conflagrations.

The Hadrianic fire of London coincided with a new
outburst of building activity in the Romano-British
towns. No doubt this represents the reaction of a generation yet more conscious of civilization and its meaning
than the second generation after the conquest. Many
towns in Gaul had taken even longer in the process of
self-Romanization. But there can be no doubt also that
the visit of Hadrian to the province, where he is recorded
to have 'set much in order,' had in the civil area an effect

no less powerful than on the northern frontier. The two scenes, military and civil, form one act. The most striking testimony comes from Viroconium (Wroxeter) on the Severn, capital of the Cornovii, where the great inscription, dedicating the city-hall and market-square of the town to Hadrian in A.D. 129–30, still wins the admiration evoked by all Roman monumental lettering. With this great building is contemporary the planned street-system, dividing at least 180 acres into spacious rectangular building-blocks, many of which were occupied by the large residences of tribal magnates. The spectacle is somewhat like the English county town of the eighteenth century, wherein important local landowners had their town-houses, used periodically when their duties as councillors or justices required a stay in town or when the family came in for a season of entertainment. Such a centre was not the crowded and pulsating town of the Mediterranean world, of which country-life was as it were a centrifugal manifestation. It was rather the product of a centripetal movement, representing the creation by the countryside of a centre for its social needs. And, although these were very different things, the outward material effects had something in common, which Italian and British landowners might have shared with mutual comprehension.

Another town in which social requirements were developing was Ratae Coritanorum (Leicester), capital of the tribe out of whose territory the *colonia* at Lindum (Lincoln) had been carved. Hadrian's work can be traced on the Fosse Way, approaching the town from Lincoln, which was now remodelled and fitted with milestones, no doubt at the expense of the Coritani both in money and compulsory labour. But in the town itself a fine suite of public baths was also being built, with a pub-

lic hall attached. By one of those mischances which are
so vividly described by Pliny in the province of Bithynia,
the line for the aqueduct feeding the establishment was
miscalculated, and water seems thereafter to have been
supplied from the adjacent river to a hand-filled cistern:
work for municipal labour, but hardly consonant with
the best standards of the day. It will suggest that the
baths were by no means in continual use, and may serve
to qualify a rosy view of universally extended social
amenities frequently enjoyed.

The clearest picture, however, of what the impulse of
the Hadrianic age meant is supplied at Verulamium (St
Albans), where the town was entirely rebuilt, partly on
and partly off the old site. The old 100-acre town, of
rhomboidal plan, was replaced by a new and roughly
oval town twice as large, with a forum more monumental
in plan and aspect than most in Britain, a small theatre,
convertible for shows as well as acting, and a market-hall.
Other public buildings no doubt await discovery, but the
balanced excavation sampled in addition a residential
quarter, in which there was a fair sprinkling of wealthy
citizens' houses. These were comfortable dwellings, in
many cases half-timbered and mostly a single story in
height, sprawling alongside or round a roomy garden-
court. They are emphatically the country dwelling
brought to town, and there is no sense of crowding or of
the tight-lined planning that goes with urban development. Those who planned the town were determined that
the gentry should have room. The shop-keepers, whose
long narrow buildings jostled one another on the main
streets, belonged to a different class, whose policy was
minimum capital expenditure combined with maximum
profit upon an outlay involving much higher risk than a
modern manufacturer or retailer would care to face.

A great defensive wall and huge dry ditch surrounded the whole town, with widely spaced projecting towers, four main gates, and several posterns. The gates are of the monumental type, with double carriage-ways and footways between semicircular towers, and they emphasize that such defences, while securing the town by night and shielding it against brigands or revolts, also reflected the pride of a tribal centre in its status. What that status was, as expressed in Roman constitutional terms, is uncertain. If a *municipium*, or chartered town, then it formed a special enclave within the tribal area, unless that area was formally attributed to it. There is no evidence for the first arrangement. The second is possible at Ratae (Leicester) but unproven elsewhere, and it may well be that the towns remained unchartered townships, or *oppida*, whose status was defined in the treaty governing the tribal relations with the provincial government. Verulamium is once described by the historian Tacitus as a *municipium*, but it is not certain that he is using the word in its strict legal sense; it was often used loosely, as a synonym for 'town'.

The relationship of the tribal aristocracy to trade and to incoming settlers from elsewhere in the Roman Empire is obscure and difficult to determine. In other regions of the Roman world land-owning and trading often went together, in the sense that a landowner would invest spare capital in a business run by his slaves. But intelligent business-trained slaves in the hands of Roman citizens, as the wealthy members of the tribal council soon became by serving in magistracies, soon graduated into freed-men, whose enterprise and ambitions all lay in the direction of trade. How many of these did a Romano-British tribal capital contain? No answer is at present possible, just as no estimate can be made of the number of Roman citizens in the form of retired soldiers or traders who settled there for business. Such folk undoubtedly existed. There was a 'gild of Roman citizens settled at Calleva' (Silchester), tribal capital of the Atrebates, which was the hub of the Roman road system to the west and south-west from London; and some of them were somehow connected with a Rhineland legion, XXI Rapax. How did these link with the Tammonii, one of the old families of the tribe, worshippers of Hercules Segomo? What, again, was the relationship between the tribal aristocracy of Venta Silurum (Caerwent) and Nonius Romanus, who was important enough to be excused his gild obligations and signalized his gratitude by a dedication to a native Mars Ocelus, whom he equated with Lenus, the war-god of the Moselle district? Such questions cannot be answered, but the fact that they can be put demonstrates the variety of the social scene and the many problems which a dearth of documentation leaves unanswered.

There is, however, another social problem upon which the scale and disposition of the tribal capitals gives some answer. Certain tribal capitals in Britain are exceptionally small. Two of these, Venta Silurum (Caerwent) and Venta Icenorum (Caister-by-Norwich), belong to tribes whose resistance to Rome had been fierce and in the former case protracted. The Iceni had begun relations with Rome as an allied client-kingdom, whose royal family and restive nobility instigated a wild revolt when the kingdom was annexed. The wasting which followed retarded economic development and crippled the tribal resources, so that Venta began to develop as a town only in the second century A.D. At Venta Silurum the tribe perhaps lost less by stubborn resistance than the Iceni lost by rebellion. At all events town-life began sooner and, although the town never grew beyond its forty-five acres and always remained unpretentious, the place reflects on smaller scale what was happening elsewhere. By the early third century A.D. it was erecting an honorary statue to a benefactor in regular Roman fashion. One tribe had no central capital. The Durotriges of Dorset, whose initial resistance to Rome had to be broken by the storming of numerous hill-forts – the Life of Vespasian mentions twenty in Wessex – were divided between two centres, at Durnonovaria (Dorchester) and Lindinae (Ilchester). This may have been due to the separation of the two areas by the Blackmore Forest (Alauna silva), just as in Gaul the Vocontii of the Vaucluse were governed from different centres in their two main valleys. But the cleavage of a tribal area is for Britain so exceptional that it is more easily regarded as an early arrangement intended to break the unity of the tribe and perhaps to facilitate its inclusion within the client kingdom of Cogidumnus.

Uniformity, however, was no Roman constitutional fetish. Indeed, nothing is more characteristic of Roman imperial development than a readiness to work within existing arrangements provided these could be assimilated to Roman form. The history of the northern tribes of Britain is an object-lesson in the handling of this principle. Those permanently included within the province were two, the far-flung Brigantes, whose lands extended from sea to sea; and the Parisi, possessors of eastern Yorkshire, thickly populated from of old. The Parisi had welcomed Roman merchants for a generation before they became part of the province in A.D. 71; and it was through their territory that the army of Cerealis carried out its main advance upon the Brigantes. That this move was peacefully received, if not welcomed, is shown by the subsequent immunity of the tribe from permanent Roman garrisons, of which only one occurs, stationed at Derventio (Malton), the north-western gate over against the Brigantes. Derventio always remained a garrisoned centre, and was much used later for the collection of grain for the army; but it may also have represented a standing insurance against an outburst of animosity between tribes. An immune area, however, where native custom reigned undisturbed, might well become a backwater: and among the Parisi the continuity of tribal institutions is reflected in their administrative arrangements. The capital, Petuaria, is still described in the middle of the second century A.D. as a *vicus*, or village-community, and the significance of this appears in its name, which in Old British means 'fourth'. There were, then, at least four such centres within the tribe, a development closely comparable with that described by Strabo as obtaining among the allied Gallic tribe of the Allobroges. They lived, he states, 'in village communities'. He adds, however, that of late the village which was their governing centre had been embellished so as to become a city. The comparison is illuminating, the more so since the Parisi did not so eagerly take the second step towards Romanization. The inscription which mentions the *vicus* of Petuaria records the erection of a theatre-stage by an *aedilis*, or junior principal magistrate, and this implies some degree of the new civility. But the place never grew into a town. Another aspect of the same picture is afforded by the countryside. The houses of farming estates on the Yorkshire wolds early became Roman in build but their owners placidly eschewed all Roman amenities until the third century A.D., preferring the ways of their forefathers consolidated, as it were, but little moderated. Here, then, is an area where Romanization came late and precisely because the inhabitants, using their freedom of choice, held aloof from the brave new world.

The wider area of the Brigantes offers potentially and exhibits in reality wider variation. The rich plain of York, which the legionary fortress of Eburacum dominated in the same way as Isca Silurum (Caerleon) watched the Glamorgan sea-plain, was the fattest region of the tribe. Here lay its eighty-acre capital, Isurium Brigantum (Aldborough), at the crossing of the Ure. Here too an increasing number of farming estates has been recognized, the homes of the tribal aristocracy. But there are many thickly populated areas where this villa-life has not yet appeared, and where town-life is either modest or non-existent. Neither Craven nor Cleveland, both heavily exploited agricultural districts, has yet afforded such manifestations. Calderdale, productive of inscriptions suggesting veteran land-settlements, seems without an urban centre. The Cumbrian sea-plain, boasting at Luguvallium (Carlisle) a town of some size and pretensions, has yielded no villa, though densely studded with native farms. The Durham magnesian limestone plateau so far exhibits one villa only, but no town. These widely separated districts do not, however, comprise the whole territory. The Pennines and their passes, all Lancashire and Westmorland, most of Cumberland, and (if it belonged to the Brigantes at all), most of Derbyshire, present a picture of lands under military occupation, policed and patrolled by permanently stationed garrisons. Here the native communities of fell and forest, tied to their flocks and herds, were kept from internecine strife and it seems that their little farms grew and spread. But neither the habit of life nor the economic level of such folk was conducive to an adoption of Roman ways. Their market needs were few and could be met either at tribal fairs or in the settlements for entertainment and trading which grew up round all but the wildest forts. So over a wide area of Brigantian territory martial law or its shadow reigned and the *pax Romana* spelt an unexciting daily life, punctuated by many duties to both tribal and central government. For the rest the pattern of the civilian areas is certainly uneven, if not always now to be descried; and it emphasizes the lack of unity and political cohesion which had originally brought upon the tribe the yoke of Roman rule. For people in this stage of development the yoke was heavy and the burden not light.

The military *vicus*, or village which grew up outside a fort, had, however, an important part to play in the economic development of northern Britain. It must from the first have formed the centre for a local market as well as ministering to the recreation of the soldiers, and development along these lines might be so promising as to tempt the serving soldier into business and eventual retirement. Most of the buildings associated with them are long narrow shops or taverns with an open front shut with sliding doors, and a large back room for goods or service. The proprietor and his family lived upon an upper floor. With the institution of land settlements for serving soldiers in the third century A.D. these extra-mural settlements became more than ever the local centres. It is clear that some were very large. On or near Hadrian's Wall the *vici* at Chesters, Chesterholm, and Housesteads covered an area larger than the fort. The Housesteads *vicus* was associated in the fourth century A.D. with a special gateway by which trade passed through the Wall to and from the territory beyond. The wide development of the *vicus* at the military supply depot at

NORTHERN
BRITAIN
IN THE THIRD
CENTURY A.D.

Figure 7

Corbridge made of it a virtual town. Air-photography at
Piercebridge (Co. Durham) or Old Carlisle (Cumberland) and past field-observation at Old Penrith (Cumberland) attest very large settlements there, where a
military road-centre supplied the traffic-routes to a
market. The substantial shops and taverns excavated in
the nineteenth century at Binchester (Co. Durham) witness a similar development for the same reasons. In Upper
Germany, as the frontier line advanced, not a few such
settlements were left without garrisons and, far from fad-
ing out of existence, continued to grow into prosperous
towns. In Britain examples of the same thing occur at
Luguvallium (Carlisle) and Caturactonium (Catterick

Bridge, Yorkshire). There are, on the other hand, many places where this development never occurred. It did not happen either in Wales, pacified though the country was, or in most lands west of the Pennines, and it is significant that the places where it occurred remained important traffic centres, related to good agricultural land.

The tribes further north, in Lowland Scotland, now within the province and now outside it, were in the former event wholly subjected to military control. A difference of treatment is discernible. The Votadini, whose territory included Northumberland and Mid-lothian, were treated in far more friendly fashion than their neighbours the Selgovae, the one territory exhibit-ing few garrisons while the other is thickly studded. A similar discrimination was probably exercised between the Damnonii and the Novantae, but is less easy to define. Control certainly extended to native settlements: the Votadini were permitted still to dwell in their hill-top town on Traprain Law, but the major hill-forts of the Selgovae show no such licence; Ruberslaw and the North Eildon stood empty and were occupied by Roman signal-stations. This pattern of control had already been exem-plified among the hill-folk of Wales and the Pennines. Many of the Welsh hill-forts are known to have been emptied of their inhabitants and rendered useless for defence. There remained, reduced to helplessness, only the farming communities which the forts had dominated. The Brigantian hill-forts met the same fate: indeed, the action of destroying these north British strongholds be-came, like the destruction of Moorish kraals, a by-word for military activity – '*dirue Maurorum attegias, castella Brigantum*'. In such areas, as on the Westmorland fells, Roman rule brought peace but hardly plenty. Yet it is well to recall that within any tribal area, however civilized the chief town and its notables or their country seats, there were many small farmers among whom the scale of prosperity, varying in some degree according to their occupation, never rose high. The small farmers or crofters provided rents and taxes for tribe and provincial government. Their lads must from time to time have had to face the conscription officer, seeking his periodical quota of army recruits. This background of toil and hard living is not wholly black, but its tones are always sombre. They throw the higher achievements into brighter relief, while emphasizing the fact that ancient polite society was not broadly based.

The foregoing review of the various British towns and cantons plainly shows that, as in Gaul, they were left to feel their own way towards a Romanization which proceeded wherever possible within native framework. It reveals also that the average British tribal notable cared more for his estates than for town-life. The great Italian landowners had sprung from the towns and made them their headquarters: and in addition to the country properties, their town-house was frequently closely related to shops or factories in which trades run by slaves and freedmen flourished. In this way wealth bred wealth. Contrariwise, the Romano-British landowner was based upon the country. For the most part the town was for him an occasional necessity rather than a permanent base of operations. But the creation of the towns does in fact show that some of the tribal gentry came to take the Roman attitude, establishing themselves in the town for at least part of the year and presumably keeping a profitable grip upon cantonal economics and local government. Tribal politics and family cliques or rivalries will have played their part in determining what proportion of the tribal aristocracy adopted these new habits. Again, those who

owned the real property of new value, such as the clay-
land for tileries, the quarries for free-stone and flagging,
the gravel for road-making, or the woods for timber, will
have been ready to profit by the new building programme. But the momentum was lacking to create a
sufficiently large steady market, except in such a centre
as London. The Romano-British towns thus tended to be
small. It is remarkable how many of them, upon receiving their walls or ramparts later in the second century
A.D., settled down at a size of round about 100 acres.
Some had unquestionably been larger. Calleva Atrebatum (Silchester) had begun ambitiously at twice the size,
Durovernum Cantiorum (Canterbury) had a large suburb
which was not included within fortifications. But Noviomagus Regnensium (Chichester), Venta Belgarum (Winchester), Ratae Coritanorum (Leicester), and Isca
Dumnoniorum (Exeter) all settled down at the 100-acre
size without sign of strain or constriction. Isurium Brigantum (Aldborough) was slightly smaller. Only Corinium
Dobunnorum (Cirencester) remained exceptionally large,
at over 200 acres, a size which puts it into the class of
Verulamium (St Albans) and Viroconium Cornoviorum
(Wroxeter). All were the capital towns of early allies and
in such communities Romanization will have proceeded
at a rapid pace amid favoured treatment. All, too, were
set in fertile territory rich in cornland, pasture, and
timber.

The only town among them all to have been fully
excavated is Calleva Atrebatum (Silchester). Allowance,
too, must be made for the fact that these excavations
were early, in many respects uncoordinated and of very
uneven quality in execution. But the overall impression
may be taken as a substantially accurate picture of a
Romano-British town of the third and fourth centuries

A.D. It contained the administrative buildings and market-place, four pagan temples and a small but central Christian church, public baths, a large *mansio* for the Imperial Post, and a fine extramural amphitheatre. The town-wall was an impressive structure, with a large fosse outside it and imposing semi-monumental gates. The

Figure 8. Calleva Atrebatum (Silchester); a typical Romano-British tribal capital

main street was lined fairly thickly with shops and work-shops. There were about twenty-five really large houses and something like the same number of small ones, the former representing the houses of tribal notables, the latter the houses of administrators or merchants. To esti-mate accurately the population of such a place is diffi-cult; it would perhaps be fair to reckon it at not less than

2500 on the showing of the plan. But if many timber
structures were missed this number may have been
doubled or even trebled. On the medium reckoning, or
even at the highest, the town was, however, no more
populous than a small market town of to-day; and, when
it is considered how highly self-sufficing country folk of
the period contrived to be, this estimate may not seem
amiss. When the houses of the governing class are related
to the cantonal council of 100 *decuriones* it might mean
that about one-quarter had come to town while the rest
remained dispersed in the canton, and this again would
not seem an unlikely figure.

The public buildings of Calleva (Silchester), in common with those of Venta Silurum (Caerwent), are of
modest architectural design. At both places the town-
hall (*basilica*) and market-place (*forum*) are combined
in a plan highly reminiscent of the legionary headquarters
building (*principia*) and thought perhaps to derive from
it. Others, however, have argued that the reverse is true.
But, whatever the original connexion, it may be regarded
as certain that the military architect had much to do
with the lay-out of British towns, since he was frequently
called in for government-sponsored work in the provinces.
At Calleva substantial use was made of Italian marble in
the decoration of the basilica, and its sculptures included
a large stone statue of the *genius, Tutela* or guardian
deity of the canton, and a large Imperial bronze statue in
armour. The Baths of Calleva are again reminiscent of
military type, though as time went on they became less
so. In this specialized field of building technique an inter-
change of civilian and military architecture is even more
likely.

It has already been noted that the status of the cantonal
capitals is uncertain. But it may be regarded as sure that

the magistrates at least would become Roman citizens upon entering office. This practice was founded upon a very ancient political custom in the Roman world by which allies of equally civilized status received the citizenship for their whole *ordo* of *decuriones*, while among those of lesser cultural achievement the privilege was confined to holders of the higher magistracies. Nor need it be doubted that upgrading will have taken place in communities at first more backward. It must be remembered that in A.D. 213 the citizenship was granted outright, except in a limited number of specified classes, to all freeborn individuals within the Empire.

The executive officers who carried out the work of the *decuriones* or *ordo splendidissimus*, as the cantonal senate was called, were few in number. There were four principal magistrates, two senior, the *duoviri iuredicundo*, and two junior, the *duoviri aediles*, all elected annually. The senior pair were concerned with the administration of justice on all civil cases below a certain value and minor criminal cases. Civil cases of high value and criminal cases involving capital punishment went to the Roman governor's courts or to his juridical deputy, the *legatus iuridicus*, which were held at assize centres (*conventus*), of which the location in Britain in unknown. All cases between Roman citizens went to Roman courts as a matter of course. The junior pair were concerned with the letting of contracts, the upkeep and repair of public buildings, or installations. Both sets of magistrates celebrated their election to office by games, entertainments, or gifts to the community in the Roman manner; an *aedilis* is seen presenting a new stage-front to the local theatre at Petuaria (Brough on Humber).

On the fiscal side the *decuriones* were legally responsible for the collection of the Roman provincial taxation in money and kind. They also determined and collected such local taxation as the tribal council saw fit to levy. They were not initially responsible, however, for the assessment of the Roman taxes, which comprised a land-tax (*tributum soli*) and a poll-tax (*tributum capitis*). These were carried out by the Roman *censitores*, or census officers, and involved the compilation of a detailed list of populace, property, produce, and animals, upon which the initial taxation was based. The first census and subsequent general revisions were carried out by a sena-torial special commissioner, of high reputation and probity. But the intermediate adjustments, rendered necessary by transfers of property, were carried out every five years by the tribal authority. For that occasion the two senior magistrates were chosen with especial care and received the title *duoviri quinquennales*, an honour valued for its indication of public trust and esteem. The revisions thus carried out would be agreed with the department of the procurator, the Imperial officer of equestrian standing stationed in London, who was responsible for the collection of the provincial taxes.

The money taxes were paid into the Imperial Treasury. The taxes in kind were delivered to the Imperial services for which they were levied. The corn-tax, for example, was mostly paid to the army authorities, and the *civitas* responsible for payment had to deliver it at the point indicated by them. Such a collecting depot was established during the first fifty years of the province at Rutupiae (Richborough), whence supplies were shipped north-wards for campaigns. But Tacitus also speaks of long and awkward deliveries, which implies direct servicing of permanent garrisons as well. The financial and physical responsibility for the task fell upon the canton concerned.

The upkeep of cantonal roads fell upon the community

also, and for such main roads as were laid out and engineered by the central government the canton was required to provide materials and labour-gangs, who would work under supervision of the Roman military engineers. These roads comprised not only the trunk roads necessary for provincial communication and strategy, but the secondary roads which opened up the territory of the canton and linked its minor administrative centres. Anyone who sees the Roman south-west road streaking through the Wiltshire and Dorset downlands to-day, with its twenty-five foot central causeway and the cleared belt defined by ditch and bank on either side of it, will get a grim idea of the work which the *civitates* had to perform. Even to-day the remains strike the eye almost as forcibly as a railway track. In addition to the construction and maintenance of the principal roads to the pattern and satisfaction of the central authorities, there was the upkeep of the Imperial Post. This elaborate service of courier-gigs, coaches, and heavy wagons was established for the use of Imperial officials. It was not, like the modern Postal service, a government institution run for the benefit of the public, but a service operated at public expense for the use of the government. The roads on which such a service ran were limited: the Antonine Itinerary, a document of the early third century A.D., with later alterations, gives a list for the whole Empire, in which Britain has sixteen routes thus equipped. Radiating from London, they serve all the cantonal capitals and cover the principal lines of penetration in the military areas. They are not always the most direct routes but they represent the principal traffic lines and are arranged in relation to the two principal fiscal centres of the time in the island, namely, London and York. As the work indicates, without differentiation, the roads were pro-

vided at about twelve-mile stages (those of the military
districts are longer) with changing-stations (*mutationes*),
where horses could be changed, and rest-houses (*mansiones*), where accommodation for the night was provided. The communities were expected to furnish and
feed sufficient horses for the traffic – requisitioning might
be resorted to in case of failure – and to keep the rest-
houses in good order, furnishing them with fuel and the
bare necessities of food. In the capital towns the rest-
houses (*mansiones*) were large and commodious structures with bath-house attached. The upkeep of all these
installations and equipment and the general cost of maintenance of vehicles, represented a substantial burden
which must have fallen very heavily upon the *civitates*
through which the heaviest traffic passed, for example,
Verulamium (St Albans), Durovernum (Canterbury), or
Calleva (Silchester).

Two sites or establishments connected with towns or
settlements fall to be described among the urban institutions of Roman Britain, although neither was a normal
town. These are the spas of Aquae Sulis (Bath) and
Aquae Arnemetiae (Buxton). Aquae Sulis, whose presiding deity was Sul Minerva, was in fact a small town of
about twenty-two acres, and its defensive wall, built in
later Roman days, embodied in its masonry many tombstones of earlier inhabitants. But all structures inside the
walls seem to have been dwarfed by the great curative
Baths, the largest of their kind known in western Europe.
The establishment as now visible seems to have been
designed originally as three great swimming-baths or
plunge-baths arranged in series, the largest, now the
Great Bath, certainly at first uncovered and flanked by
well-proportioned colonnades with alcoves. The water
issues from a very deep and copious natural spring, at the

high temperature of 120° Fahrenheit, and thus offers pleasant bathing apart from its curative properties, beneficial in cases of rheumatic and scrofulous complaints. If there also existed as part of the original concern hot baths of the everyday kind, dissociated from spas, their position is unknown. But later these appear at both ends of the building and exhibit many signs of repeated renewal and alteration. The Great Bath was also altered and improved by being roofed across by a great tunnel vault, with large open lunettes at each end, reminiscent of a railway station, from which the steam could escape. This huge vault, some thirty-five feet in span, demanded a massive strengthening of the portico piers, which were used to carry it, while the portico and its niches were converted by cross-ribbed arches into veritable flying buttresses, bringing the stresses down to earth. The highly ambitious and luxurious architectural scheme, which brought to Britain an example of thoroughly experienced Roman architecture, has not received the attention which it deserves.

No less notable are the architectural details. The outstanding pieces are the pediment and associated columns, capitals and entablature belonging to the temple of Sul Minerva. The pediment, with its remarkable shield supported by flying Victories, is mentioned elsewhere (p. 102). But it may be remarked here that the capitals and entablature rank with the best sculpture of the Three Gauls and remind us that sculptors from the Chartres district were at work in Bath. The Wall of the Four Seasons, dedicated by officials of a gild, is a conventional piece of architectural panelling, but the figured panels are endowed with both grace and vigour. There are also seen some notable decorated mouldings from a free-standing monument with four niches set back to back in pairs; while the coping designed as a mastiff biting a stag is one of those pieces of provincial art in which Roman and medieval craftsmen seem to approach one another across the Dark Age which divided them. It is not the only piece of its kind at Bath. There is an oddly medieval air about the pewter stag which serves as a candelabrum. Less anticipatory but no less curious is the large pewter mask or metope figuring a deity with painted beard and moustache and native style of hair-dressing: this is an old god of sea and water, comparable with the occupant of the great pedimental shield, Manwydd or his like, of whom Sul Minerva, the goddess of the sacred spring, was presumably a daughter. Sul Minerva herself is represented by a famous bronze head, commented upon elsewhere in this chapter (p. 108). The Roman spa at Bath is, in short, not only remarkable among the architectural remains of Roman Britain, but more than holds its own in comparison with other curative establishments in the Roman world, as is evident from known plans. The Romans themselves were not, however, interested in this point: for them the most notable thing about these 'richly adorned baths' was the curious fuel used upon the altars of the goddess, 'which did not waste away but turned to stony lumps'. This was the Somersetshire coal, a freakish fuel to Roman experience in general, though in fact coal was much used in Roman Britain (see p. 159).

In contrast with the notable relics and substantial information available concerning Aquae Sulis, the Buxton waters, Aquae Arnemetiae, afford all too little evidence of their Roman use. There is a reliable statement that lead-lined baths, associated with Roman structures, were seen in the late seventeenth century and further remains in 1780, all close to St Anne's well. St Anne herself may, indeed, well be the Christian version of Arnemetia, the patron goddess of the spring in Roman days, whose name is Celtic and means 'She who dwelt over against the sacred grove'. For the rest, the site had been, like Bath, in Roman military occupation during its earliest days, when its tepid waters were no doubt first observed. But, unlike Bath, it always remained on the fringe of the military area. In this it resembles such places as Wiesbaden (Aquae Mattiacorum) or Badenweiler, which lay close behind the military zone of Roman Germany, and attracted a numerous public of both soldiers and civilians. The social pleasures of such spas counted for at least as much as their curative qualities, and they were pleasant resorts for soldiers or officials on leave or for civilians on holiday.

The smaller centres within tribal territories have already been mentioned in connexion with the great roads. From the tribal point of view the most important were those which perpetuated the ancient organization of the territory. Celtic tribes were divided, for purposes of local government and for the raising of warrior bands, into *pagi* or *curiae*; and in some Continental tribes the *pagus* was retained as a basis for army recruitment in the service of Rome. Whatever its title, however, the local unit of territory, with its local magistrates, performed on a smaller and still more limited scale the functions of the tribal magistrates in the cantonal capital. Such units, too, were of importance in fiscal organization, particularly in relation to the collection of taxes in kind; and this explains the interest of the Roman government in seeing that they were linked by the main road system. The little that is known about the internal arrangement of such townships is due to air-photography. It is clear that they were loosely planned, usually spreading out irregularly from the main road that passed through them. Accordingly, the plan of their walls is seldom regular: Kenchester is an irregular hexagon, Chesterton an ovoid, Alchester and Dorchester (Oxon) are sub-rectangular. But Alchester contained something like a little *forum*, if it was not a temple-precinct: Kenchester possessed a fine bath building and some houses embellished with sumptuous patterned mosaic pavements. All possessed numerous shops and workshops, indicative of their importance as local market centres; and these conformed to the normal type with narrow frontage and much depth and an upper storey for the proprietor's dwelling. Some towns were the stations of Imperial officials: Dorchester (Oxon.) housed a *beneficiarius*, a military officer seconded to special duty often in connexion with road and river traffic or tax-collecting or both; at Irchester, amid rich horse-pastures, was quartered a *strator*, or remount officer. Facts of this kind demonstrate collectively that these small places had their own part to play in the administration of the canton and in the wider ramifications of Imperial taxation, but their remains are for the most part eloquent of modern neglect rather than ancient history.

It follows, however, that, for the sake of ensuring the safe-keeping of the administrative and local taxation-records or stores contained within these small places, the provincial government saw to it that such centres were walled. Examples of the kind are the Oxfordshire centres of Alchester and Dorchester, the Northamptonshire Irchester, the Lincolnshire Horncastle and Caistor on the Wolds, Kenchester in Herefordshire, Chesterford in Essex, Caister by Yarmouth in Norfolk, Catterick and Norton in Yorkshire. Norton was one of the *pagus* centres of the Parisi, while Kenchester and Catterick lay on Imperial post-roads. But the other examples here selected have been chosen for their connexion with bye-roads, lest they should be confused with the posting-stations associated with arterial routes. Many of these stations, presumably the *mansiones*, were also walled; and some were local road-centres of such importance that they must be regarded as performing a double function. Good examples of this sort on the trunk roads are Rochester (Kent), Towcester (Northamptonshire), Baldock (Hertfordshire), Great Casterton (Rutland), Chesterton (Northamptonshire), Wall (Staffordshire), Mildenhall (Wiltshire), and Droitwich (Worcestershire). By contrast, there were important road-junctions where no settlement of any importance appears to have existed; Badbury in Dorset, Old Sarum in Wiltshire, and High Cross in Leicestershire are striking cases. Examples abound of walled posting-stations which can hardly be considered large enough to rank as *pagus*-centres, and there may be instanced Penkridge (Staffordshire), Mancetter (Leicestershire), Ancaster and Littleborough (Lincolnshire), Leintwardine (Herefordshire), and East Stoke (Nottinghamshire).

The provision of defensive walls for all these centres might seem to indicate that the province was unusually troubled by raiders or by outbursts of local unrest. But in the Roman Empire this emphasis upon fortification of critical points was normal. In the absence of an effectively co-ordinated police force, it was important to ensure in advance that opportunities for brigandage or local peasant risings were eliminated by securing travellers' rests and local administrative or fiscal centres against them. That brigandage was in general effectively checked and restrained – its punishment by crucifixion or laceration by wild beasts was sufficiently severe – is attested by the open and carefree villa system obtaining all over the province. But prevention came before cure, and this explains conditions which look at first sight almost like a contradiction in terms.

The responsibilities of local government and increasing fiscal burdens tended in the later Empire to convert the decurionate, as membership of the tribal council was called, from an honour to an anxiety. But in the earlier Empire it was a prized distinction and an object of family ambition and rivalry. In Gaul, where such rivalry (*aemulatio*) laid the foundations of the French *émulation*, the effect was to run communities into heavy expenditure upon building programmes, financed both from public funds and private pockets. In Britain there must have been something of this, but it cannot be claimed as an outstanding feature of Romano-British town-life. This contrast is plainly due to a different attitude in Britain towards Romanization and its implications, and it has been held by notable authorities that it was based upon the relative poverty of British cantons as compared with the Gallic *civitates*. But, if the Gallic manifestation of public spirit was due to an outlook characteristic of the province, it should not be forgotten that Tacitus cited certain peculiarities native to Britain; and prominent among these was the habit, no less clearly ancestral than *émulation*, of acquiescence in taxes and demands, so long as justice was observed. It may be asked what effect, as compared with Gaul, such an attitude may have had upon the relations between British landowners and their tenants, or upon cantonal taxation? If the exactions of the great Gallic landlords tended to provoke their tenantry to revolt and outlawry, British landlords were presumably held by public opinion to fairer conditions, which resulted in less wealth and therefore less opportunity or temptation to give way to family or cantonal rivalries. The moderating effect of such an attitude upon

both cantonal building programmes and private muni-
ficence would produce a world which was more drab yet
more kindly, and lives that were more humdrum yet
more humane. It is perhaps, then, no accident that the
difference in mode between the provincial characters
matches the contrast in outward show. It may also well
explain why in the second century, when taxation and
exactions had not yet become a pressing public evil, the
British landowners did not base themselves in large
numbers upon the town as well as the country. Absentee
landlordism did not suit the pockets of the majority.

The effect of this restrained indulgence in the attrac-
tions of town-life was not, however, everywhere the same,
nor did it remain constant. A striking case is provided by
Verulamium, where excavation showed that the residential quarter, which was so prosperous in the second
century A.D., became ramshackle in the extreme by the
close of the third. This decline may represent not so much
the failing fortunes of the town as curtailment by rural
capitalists of the least binding of their obligations. When
confidence was restored by the new government of Constantius, and opportunity by the actual presence of the
Caesar, not only did the residential quarter take on a new
lease of life, but considerable sums of cantonal or private
money were spent upon the erection, restoration, or
enlargement of public buildings. The residential and public activity go together, for the spending of money upon
contracts and materials attracted again to town those
owners of real estate to whom the spending of money on
public works meant profits. It should be remarked that
all the known building on a grand scale is concerned
with public amenities: the theatre is enlarged and
embellished, the market-hall is rebuilt in new style, and
the road between them is spanned by a triumphal arch.

Politically, it no doubt implied a new programme of self-advertisement on the part of those who had not been prominent supporters of the recent usurper régime, and it may well represent new blood in cantonal politics and new opportunities in public life.

This quite notable revival on the spectacular side of town-life did not last long. Three generations later the theatre was in complete decay and most of the private houses inhabited by folk who had no care for their decorations. The fate of the theatre was positively start-ling. The area in front of the stage was gradually buried many feet deep in tipped rubbish, high in vegetable con-tent, containing many thousands of the insignificant coins of the last quarter of the fourth century A.D.; and such a deposit can hardly represent anything but the sweeping or periodic cleaning of trodden refuse from a market area, where large quantities of small change were continually passing. Thus, although Verulamium had lost its theatrical performances – and áscendant Christian feeling of the period would have deemed this gain rather than loss – it retained its importance as a market centre. This state of affairs must in fact have continued into the third decade of the fifth century A.D., when St Germanus was able to meet the notables of the town, in order to correct their heretical tendencies, and found them in a state of prosperity. The evidence thus comes into perspec-tive. The residential quarter of the town had in fact been decaying; but it is not to be supposed that the notables in splendid raiment who met St Germanus lived in hovels and spent all their money upon their backs. They must have represented, as tradition would demand, the can-tonal magnates assembled for the purpose. The town around them, however, was not deserted. Its prosperity was concentrated in the shops and workshops which have so far remained unexcavated. The environment of these, as the archaeology of any medieval city will show, might be squalid indeed, and the town none the less prosperous. Accordingly the picture of decay based upon material evidence applies to certain phases of town-life only and not to all its essential elements. If the tribal notables had ceased to make town-life a cultural factor in their lives, there were still many lesser folk who found the town and, above all, its protective ring of walls, a source and condition of mercantile livelihood and profit.

This change in the character of the Romano-British towns was not confined to the cantonal capitals. The *colonia* of Lindum (Lincoln), founded at the close of the first century A.D., had begun its existence as a chartered town of privileged discharged soldiers, mostly legionaries. Living in a small and rigidly planned town of some forty acres, and initially supported by grants of money and of land in the vicinity, they formed from the first a community attractive to traders and ready to invest in commercial enterprises. The town thus grew, and at the opening of the third century A.D. received an extension to its walls which more than doubled its size. This brought Lindum down-hill to the Witham and to the associated canals between the Fens and the Trent. At this peak of prosperity, as excavations have shown, the lower town contained handsome and lavishly decorated buildings extending some distance behind the main street. But in the fourth century A.D. the buildings in question were totally dismantled and their sites were occupied by modest structures of non-monumental character, later honeycombed in turn by medieval cess-pits. This decline in splendour would seem to imply that in late-Roman Lincoln the same factors were operating as in the cantonal capitals. The monumental quality of the place, which had been the pride of its founders and their successors, was submerged in a flood of traders' establishments, whether shops or workshops.

Another town in which the decay of public buildings did not spell an end to all prosperity was Viroconium (Wroxeter). This place had originally grown up out of a military trading settlement, to which had been transferred, at a date not yet established, the governing centre of the Cornovii. It is by no means the only site in Britain where a native capital came to occupy, presumably by governmental ordinance, an erstwhile Roman military site. Corinium Dobunnorum (Cirencester) and Isurium Brigantum (Aldborough) are proved examples: Ratae Coritanorum (Leicester) is almost certainly another; and in every case the determining factor was certainly the ready-made system of communications which the Roman military engineer, employing troops and the tribal *corvée*, had already provided. At Viroconium the ribbon-development of traders' shops along the main road created, as originally at Verulamium, the main street of the town. As at Verulamium also, though upon much less substantial evidence, the town is thought to have begun with earthwork defences, enclosing about 100 acres. Certain it is that under Hadrian, in the years A.D. 129–30, there was dedicated the large market-place and town-hall of the enlarged town, 180 acres in size. This town, of which large areas are well known from air-photography, is noteworthy for the substantial number of sumptuous town-houses; and there can be no doubt of the fillip which the visit of Hadrian to the province in A.D. 121 and his subsequent interest had given to Romanization among the governing classes of the Cornovii. But later days brought with them two successive blows to civic pride. In the later second century A.D. the market-place and town-hall were burnt down. In A.D. 296, when the fortress at Chester was also destroyed, the same buildings were involved in a second fire and never again reconstructed. Throughout the fourth century A.D. this principal site lay derelict and occupied by booths and workshop-shacks, while the community presumably used as civic offices the market-like building across the street. Yet other amenities had not disappeared. Adjacent to the market-hall lay the town baths, a modest but not incommodious suite, to which the hall-like building may once, as at Ratae (Leicester), have formed a social entrance hall or foyer. These Baths lasted in good working order until the eighties of the fourth century A.D., when the military occupation of Chester came to an end and ceased to provide the necessary shield from Irish raids. During all this period, however, and even after the Baths in turn had been destroyed, the shops on the main street continued to function and prosper. In the end the wheel of fortune seems indeed to have come full circle, as if the town finished its existence as it began, by ribbon development of traders along the arterial road. More information is, however, needed as to the fate of the large houses. One, near the main street, continued to be occupied in fair order until the eighties. Here there may be an indication of contrast with Verulamium. If barbarian raids had already become serious in the north-west by the close of the third century A.D., their effect may have been to drive the owners of estates into the shelter of the walled town. As between the devil of Roman tax-collection and the deep sea of barbarism, they may have chosen the evil which they knew better. The effect of such a choice would be to add to the trades population the cantonal magnates, whose estates would be run by bailiffs, taking the risk of raids but not offering as hostages to fortune the wealth or the attractive slaves of a well-appointed country house. As will appear below, when country estates are discussed, examples exist of country houses where something like a flight from the country might be thought to have taken place. At Isurium Brigantum this almost certainly happened. The large and wealthy houses have produced mosaic pavements, of which the style is not earlier than the fourth century A.D., while those in the northwest quarter of the town, which are reconstructed and late, are associated with fourth-century coins. It would seem, therefore, that the fourth-century town housed a substantial number of cantonal magnates, differing in this respect from Verulamium.

Structural evidence concerning the quality of later-Roman social life in the extensively excavated towns of Calleva (Silchester) and Venta Silurum (Caerwent) is almost completely lacking. The excavators, reaping their harvest from the lower levels, paid little attention to the top layers, which afforded more fragmentary if no less precious evidence for the latest history of these towns. Although recent excavation at Caerwent has furnished evidence of late fourth-century trading and manufacturing activity on the main street, the picture afforded is hardly large enough to form the basis for general inference. But both towns yielded so large a quantity of late fourth-century coins, including copies based upon them or clipped coinage, and Silchester in particular so much late fourth-century pottery, that there can be no doubt of a vigorous town-life in both places, whatever social elements composed it. At Venta Silurum (Caerwent), indeed, the buildings of the town had always been simple and unpretentious. Not only is the size of the place and the scale of its buildings small, but the principal houses, if provincial-Roman in plan, were most modestly equipped. Mosaic pavements and heated rooms were rare and bath-suites still rarer. 'Comfort without luxury' was the Silurian fashion, and must be regarded as reflecting the lower economic standards of a canton possessing much upland territory and forest, not to mention their thirty years' initial hostility to Rome.

Another development, however, must have taken place of which archaeology has yet afforded little evidence. As these communities became isolated in the fifth century A.D. and as the lands about them became less safe, they must have depended increasingly for their food-supply upon local harvests. A story has in fact survived of the timely relief of famine in sixth-century Isca Dumnoniorum (Exeter) by the arrival of a storm-driven corn-ship. It has been suggested with great likelihood that the Dark-Age system of dykes on the approaches to Calleva (Silchester) in fact indicates the limits of the lands upon which the food-supply of the town depended and which it was vital to conserve. Something of the same kind has been postulated for London and the similarity between the two systems is certainly close. If this interpretation be correct, Britain has yielded archaeological evidence of a stage in urban devolution rare indeed and precious to the historian.

As the picture of Romano-British urban civilization emerges, sometimes light and often dark, it becomes clear that the whole composition must have been flat and uninspired when compared with the cities in southern Europe or even with many towns north of the Cevennes. There are, moreover, certain concrete particulars in which more than a general comparison can be made. Two very closely connected material achievements of Roman civilization are sewerage and water-supplies. It is certain that in Britain, as in Gaul, the majority of cantonal capitals did not possess a general sewerage system. Sewers are entirely absent at Calleva (Silchester), where the Baths, for example, have their own special outflow unconnected with any general scheme. Venta Silurum (Caerwent) and Venta Icenorum (Caister-by-Norwich) both exhibit the same deficiency, though all these towns had a chess-board plan of streets. Nor has chance excavation ever hinted at the existence of any system of the kind in other cantonal centres. But at Lindum (Lincoln), constructed by Roman contractors for Roman ex-servicemen colonists, there is an elaborate system of main sewers with man-holes and feeders, which was laid down over an area somewhat larger than that of the *colonia* when walled. This brings Lindum into line with the principal cities of the Empire. No record exists of a similar system at Camulodunum (Colchester) or Glevum (Gloucester), which so closely resembles Lindum in other features: but this does not disprove its possible existence at either place.

Water supplies are better attested, but no example is known of the grandiose aqueducts which fed distant springs to so many Roman towns. An obvious candidate for such a scheme would be Londinium (London). Lindum, however, boasted a very remarkable water-supply, pumped up to the town from springs lying to the north-east through a rare type of water-main comprising tile pipes very heavily jacketed in concrete. The main apparently possessed at least one branch serving the extended town, but within the walls nothing is known of distributive methods. Several cantonal capitals, on the other hand, were served by a gravity supply carried below ground in timber pipes united by iron collars, which have appeared at Calleva Atrebatum (Silchester), Venta Silurum (Caerwent), and Venta Icenorum (Caister-by-Norwich). This type of conveyance was much favoured by military engineers, for the obvious reason that the pipe-line was hidden from sight below ground, and numerous examples of such systems are associated with Roman fortresses and forts in Britain, as in other frontier provinces. For urban use the disadvantage of such installations is the need for apparatus, such as buckets, pumps, or water-wheels, to raise the water to a convenient level after it has reached its terminal distribution-tank. Another type of supply is the open leet or water-course, of which an example nine miles long fed Durnonovaria (Dorchester, Dorset), while a duct of a similar kind seems to have been planned for Ratae (Leicester), but failed, as such projects sometimes did, owing to lack of skill in levelling. Such open conduits are also known to the military, and are matched on Hadrian's Wall at Aesica (Greatchesters). Only Viroconium (Wroxeter) furnishes evidence for a supply reaching the town at a height sufficient to serve lead and timber pipelines for private distribution and an overflow (*aqua caduca*) for a street-side leet, comparable with Hobson's Conduit in Cambridge. The Wroxeter leet was here and there tapped by sluices for flushing private latrines. The system is thus sufficiently developed to afford special supplies of both drinking-water and flushing-water to privileged folk. In this respect Viroconium is as far advanced as most Roman towns, where supplies were conceived as intended first for public fountains, then for Baths and only thereafter, as availability might dictate, for the private consumer.

In respect of its public water supplies, Britain thus compares not so ill with other frontier provinces, though it falls far short of the best Mediterranean standards. Other bases of comparison are hard to find, though artistic material provides highly interesting information. Here it may be remarked that, although the amount of Romano-British public art is small, its paucity must be related to the continuity of habitation and consequent destruction of Roman levels which is a feature of most of the important town-sites in Britain. Among surviving works, the bronze heads from life-sized statues of Claudius, originally from Camulodunum (Colchester), or of Hadrian, from Londinium (London), are not first-class works; but they are good examples of the class of statue commissioned by provincial centres, and hold their own with other provincial works of the kind. The York head in stone of Constantine, on the other hand, is a highly notable piece of work by any standard for its power and style: weathered though it is, it has not lost the freshness and virility of touch which is its outstanding characteristic. First among portraits of Constantine in date, it takes a first place among them for its dramatic force. Among cult-statues, Sul Minerva from Bath, goddess of Aquae Sulis, is a positively attractive piece, with a firm classic restraint worthy of a Pre-Raphaelite studio. The shield emblazoned pediment from her temple is a bold and original treatment of a hackneyed design which lifts it out of the commonplace into the realm of vigorous and sensitive art. From what is known of this public work and its quality, the province in its hey-day cannot be held lacking either in public taste or the means to gratify it, and its standards of taste cannot be dismissed as negligible.

CHAPTER THREE

THE COUNTRYSIDE

ROMAN villas are so old and well-established a part of Romano-British archaeology that they require, paradoxically, some explanation. Most have been recognized, and many rendered famous, through the discovery of their mosaic pavements, which by modern standards would belong to sumptuous country houses. But while country houses erected for pleasure existed in the Roman world, they were almost exclusively the privilege of the very wealthy. The normal Roman villa was not a liability of this kind but a profit-making farm, and the very richest villas in Roman Britain show no departure from this economic basis. Comfortable on the average, luxurious at best, and squalid at worst, the Romano-British villas ranged in size from cottage to mansion, and the associated acreage varied accordingly. Nor are villas to be connected with Roman immigrants rather than native Britons. Roman settlers there were, retired soldiers or administrators, but these were very much in a minority compared with the native British land-owners, the principal farmers and notables of the tribes. In short, the villas mostly represent the adoption of Roman standards in greater or lesser degree by natives of substance.

But it is hardly to be considered that in building villas, any more than in erecting towns, the native began on a sumptuous scale. The first villas, like the first towns, must have been, with due exceptions, simple and unpretentious houses; and three examples, two from the territory of the Catuvellauni and one from among the Belgae, will serve to illustrate the point. Park Street near St Albans and Lockleys near Welwyn began their existence as a single range of four or five rooms, divided by a passage from back to front. Park Street had a basement storehouse at one end, but neither building appears to have had a substantial upper storey. Catsgore (Somersetshire) is even simpler, comprising little more than a couple of detached barns, perhaps sub-divided in timber. In this it closely resembles the earliest Roman buildings at Langton (E. Yorks). But all three houses were erected on the site of earlier native huts, two of oblong plan at Park Street, and single round huts at Lockleys and Catsgore. Thus, however simple the new houses of Roman structure, there was a profound difference in solidity and comfort between them and the native buildings whose place they took, and the cost of making the change doubtless represented a considerable capital expenditure in the owners' eyes. As for standards, it is instructive to compare these plans with that of the smaller English farm-house of the sixteenth or seventeenth century. The types compare so closely that the known simple standards of the English example might serve as a pattern for those of earlier days. The important point about all these villas is that Roman building fashions, though not yet Roman luxury, had been adopted within a generation of the conquest.

The materials used in such houses were not necessarily the most solid and permanent. Stone foundations may connote half-timber superstructures rather than a building wholly of stone. At Ditchley (Oxfordshire), the timber posts forming a colonnade in front of the earliest house plainly indicate this type of modest structural programme, comparable with the now rare but once common timber arcades of Norman domestic architecture, of which carpentry made a delightful thing. Behind this front the

Figure 9. Ditchley, a Romano-British farm (*villa*)

Ditchley house differed little from Lockleys or Park Street, and it is probable that only a loft-like first floor rose above the colonnade. But about the turn of the first century A.D. there were added a new stone-built veranda and projecting end rooms which gave to the establishment both privacy and a new elegance. There was now room for recreation and entertainment in what had been previously a workaday farm, wherein the whole household lived together. Socially speaking, the new plan divided the household and accentuated the position of master and mistress. In Britain this type of house became widespread, and it brought the new province into touch with the mainstream of contemporary West-European domestic architecture. For in Gaul or the Rhineland the design was generally common, and went with a sizeable farm. And so it was in Britain, for on the basis of its granary accommodation the Ditchley villa has been related to an estate of some thousand acres. This supplies, then, a kind of yardstick, however rough, by which the size and standing of different kinds of villas can be gauged. Even allowing for the fact that, on the ancient system of crop-rotation, one-third of the arable lay fallow each year, it becomes clear that by this standard the numerous bigger villas must have been related to very substantial estates indeed. Not enough is known about the social organization of such larger estates to say whether they were run by slaves or by crofter-labourers. But where a resident staff of labourers appears, their accommodation nearly always takes the form of a barn-dwelling, frequently ranged on one side of a farmyard or court. This structure, convenient for so many purposes, is planned with nave and aisles divided by timber columns. As in Friesian farm-houses to-day, the nave served for stores, tools, and livestock, while the aisles or the whole of one end of the building were partitioned to house the workers. In the form of a subsidiary building essential to the working of a farm this type of house was so general, even in the largest establishments, that its prototype has been sought in the pre-Roman days. But no proof of such antecedents has yet appeared, and it may well be that the type is borrowed from the Italian *villa rustica*. There are some villas also in which this type of house is the only domestic accommodation present, as for example Clanville (Hampshire) or Denton (Lincolnshire). These represent either small tenant farms or bailiff-run establishments, where the distinction between tenant or supervisor and workers was less sharply defined. Some, as at Castlefield (Hampshire), are so primitive in their arrangements that any distinction seems out of the question.

The planning of the houses so far described is determined by work. No mention has been made of bath-houses, because in the earlier Romano-British villas of this class they are a luxury rarely supplied. It is, indeed, one of the evidences of advancing civilization that in most later villas a bath-house, however simple, is an essential part of the plan. The next class of house on the upward scale, the so-called corridor house, is a development of the Park Street type of house, by adding to the number of rooms, and linking them with a front corridor. A bath-house was often attached to one end, or set closely adjacent to avoid the risk of fire. In such houses there is a tendency for the main rooms to lie at the end of the range, but a single large central room also tends to come into prominence. This is the dining-room, the social centre of Roman private life, bracketed by Tacitus with baths as the hallmark of civility; and it must be understood that in educated Roman circles the meal was savourless without good conversation and literary entertainment. A plan of this kind is accordingly the silent witness of the adoption of such standards by British well-to-do circles. But there are also corridor houses of which the planning is still more deliberately balanced, with rooms disposed in relation to garden or landscape. Such villas, as at Folkestone with its Channel view, though not necessarily very large, evoke a picture of yet another kind of sensibility.

The conversion of a corridor-house into a courtyard house is dictated by size of household and estate rather than by other cultural or aesthetic considerations. The courtyard house always gives an impression of great size, and it is possible nowadays to exaggerate this, when so much that would now be arranged in storeys was in Roman Britain spread out upon the ground floor. Nevertheless, the biggest of these villas were large indeed, and it must be borne in mind that in a society based upon slavery or small tenants, even moderately wealthy folk tended to accumulate large households. Britain has not furnished such scenes of daily life as grace the funeral monuments of the Moselle valley in lively variety. But there is no reason to think that the life of the wealthy in the provinces differed in its essentials. So the kitchen scenes of Gallia Belgica, with their cooks and scullions, the hunting scenes, with grooms and estate lads, or the boudoir scenes, with mistress and maids, might be applied to the world of the large Romano-British villas almost without observing the change of locality. What must be emphasized, however, as a social fact, upon which stress has already been laid, is that a villa so large as Woodchester, where by no means all the remains have yet been uncovered, comprises both residential and workaday quarters. The inner garden court, with its vast house, enormous central dining-room, and imported marble sculptures, is reached through an outer courtyard flanked by a pair of barn-dwellings of the type associated with farm-workers and farm-stock. The direct connexion of this richest of houses with the development of an estate is thus demonstrated by the plan.

Woodchester was uncovered and published in an age

Figure 10. Bignor, the centre of a great estate

when evidence for the growth or evolution of villas was not sought. To perceive such a phenomenon it is necessary to go to a later excavation at Northleigh (Oxfordshire). This great house in its final form comprised a vast courtyard house of many rooms, with servants' quarters and baths occupying the two wings. The farm buildings have been descried by air-photography on a site outside the courtyard. But excavation further demonstrated that the house began its existence as a simple corridor-house with modest bath-house adjoining, covering about one-third of the later area but plainly connected with the farm. This change in the character of the main house is important as indicating the growing wealth and prosperity of the estate and its owners. The process is matched in greater or lesser degree in many villas. There are few which did not grow in prosperity, even from small beginnings: and this is something to put beside the decay of cultivated town life, which appears to blight the province and to stamp it as unfruitful.

But not all villas passed through the same kind of development. An instructive contrast is provided by Llantwit Major, in the Glamorganshire sea-plain. This estate developed in the second century A.D., administered from a simple courtyard house with modest farm-buildings attached, of which the most important was a barn-dwelling for the estate staff. At the beginning of the fourth century A.D. the main house was deserted, and fell into ruin. The barn-dwelling, on the other hand, functioned actively for another century; and it becomes evident that the estate continued to exist as an economic unit, but that its owners no longer dwelt there. Whether they had migrated behind town walls in times of uncertainty, or whether, for example, failure in the male line had transferred the estate to another family, cannot be revealed by the plan. The modifications evident in the plan of Chedworth (Gloucestershire) reveal that something like the second event certainly happened there: for this large and comfortable villa, delightfully situated and handsomely planned, was converted in its latest days into a manufactory, engaged partly in fulling cloth and partly in the production of wrought-iron agricultural tools. Such a revolution in the function of the building must have coincided with the passing of the estate into the hands of an owner who lived elsewhere and was no longer interested in its residential possibilities. The very existence of such manufacturing processes, on the other hand, is intimately connected with servicing the surrounding arable estates and the sheep-farms producing woollen cloth; and it is a likely assumption that the property had fallen into the hands of a magnate connected with one side or the other and possessed of the capital required to reap advantage from both. Comparable conversions of good farming property into manufacturing concerns have been noted at Titsey (Surrey) and Darenth (Kent); and both of these establishments are somehow connected with processing in vats, though the exact nature of the operation remains uncertain.

Normally the social picture implied by the planning of large villas is not unkindly. The master's house is flanked with quarters for servants or slaves which were not so sordid as to merit concealment. Nearly all, however, are associated with the practice of infant exposure, repellent to modern civilized folk, to a degree suggestive of a slave or serf population whose increase was harshly limited. This phenomenon is particularly marked at Hambleden (Buckinghamshire), where a small but comfortable farm overlooks an area honeycombed with successive corn-drying ovens in every variety of form, and flanked by simple barn-dwellings. The occupants of the house later reversed its main front, so that it now looked away from the work-yard, as if this had become too much of an eye-sore. It is tempting to recognize here a slave-run establishment engaged in corn-production on a large scale and managed, whether for a rich proprietor or for the Imperial Government, by a prosperous freedman bailiff.

It would be difficult in the present state of knowledge to say where villa-life began to flourish on a wide-spread scale, but it may be recognized that in some districts its beginnings came much later than others. A remarkable case of a late start occurs in the territory of the Parisi in east Yorkshire. Here, at the excavated villas of Langton and Rudston, the agricultural ditches which mark the first phase in the history of the site are strewn with pottery belonging to the late first century A.D. In other words, they mark the new phase of activity in cultivation stimulated by the *pax Romana* and by the demands of taxation or levies in kind made upon an allied community by the Roman government. But the first modest buildings in the Roman manner at both sites do not come into existence until the third century A.D. This again marks the incorporation of the tribe within the newly constituted province of Britannia Inferior and the more insistent development of the natural resources within easy range of its new capital at York. But amenities can hardly be said to exist until the fourth century A.D., by which time the still greater insistence upon the development of local economy and the ever-growing tendency to levy taxation in kind rather than in money, caused a rise in values and prices of agricultural produce and increased the wealth of farming folk. The two villas could then be furnished with mosaic pavements and bath-houses, the latter of real luxury at Rudston. Vigorous local schools of

mosaic workers, copying classical models with enthusias-
tic infidelity, grew up to meet the demand. A house of
considerable architectural pretensions at Harpham belongs to this period, though its beginnings were earlier.

A second area where development came late is the
north-east corner of the territory of the Brigantes, now
County Durham. The villa at Old Durham has a bath-
house which belongs to the fourth century A.D., and large
threshing-floors of the same date. But the agricultural
ditches which, as at Langton or Rudston, mark the earliest dated phase of activity on the site, yielded Antonine
pottery. This is interesting because it marks a forward
movement of Romanized property-holders in corres-
pondence with the advance of the Roman frontier from
the Tyne to the Forth.

There is no indication that the Old Durham site out-
lasted the severe troubles of A.D. 367–9, when Hadrian's
Wall fell and was reorganized in so different a fashion
from ever before. Open settlements so far north hardly
seem to have been regarded as safe. But the villas of the
Yorkshire Wolds lasted, behind their new coastal signal-
stations and naval protection, until at least the opening
of the fifth century A.D.: and the silver hoards of clipped
siliquae which formed the money of account in the first
decades of that century reach as far north as the Fylde
and the Tees. The peasant militia of Hadrian's Wall may
have faded out as an effective frontier force, but the inner
territory of the Brigantes was still intact and Roman,
although the central government of the Empire was no
longer in control of it. The same can be said of the coin
evidence from Britain further south, and there is a very
large number of villas which have produced coinage as
late as the close of the fourth century A.D. The Somersetshire villas have long been cited as productive of a strik-

ing number of late fourth-century silver coin-hoards; and this special phenomenon has a special explanation related to the silver-lead mines (p. 151). But the association of late coinage with villas is not confined to Somersetshire and is true of many sites south-east of a line drawn from east Yorkshire to Devon.

This evidence may seem to disregard or contradict the fact that a considerable number of sites cannot be shown to have survived for so long. There are numerous villas, widely dispersed, from which the recorded coins do not go beyond the fifties and sixties of the fourth century A.D.; and, while negative evidence of this kind may always lie open to revision, there must be some substantial truth behind this apparent termination of activity, as Haverfield long ago perceived. It must in fact have a connexion with the troublous years which culminated in the invasions of A.D. 367–9, when the province was beset on all sides by raiders from overseas and much damage was done. It would, however, be a mistake to exaggerate the permanent effect of these years of ill fortune. In east Yorkshire, for example, the damage done at Langton was repaired and an age of prosperous activity ensued. In Lincolnshire an entirely new villa at East Denton came into being after A.D. 369, and although it is of the barn-dwelling type and therefore perhaps a bailiff-run farm rather than an owner's residence, its creation nevertheless attests that confidence in the peace and potential prosperity of the countryside still reigned. At Great Casterton a villa in open country was being actively reconstructed in the eighties. It might be guessed that what caused the ultimate collapse of the villa system was not the insecurity of the countryside so much as the collapse of the world upon whose markets they had depended.

No consideration of villas as a whole is complete with-

Tombstone of Thracian cavalry-man from Gloucester, riding down a western Briton: an episode of the early days of conquest. [p. 25]

Borcovicium (Housesteads) with Hadrian's Wall and military way, looking W. *Crown Copyright* [p. 48]

(*a*) Scythes and mower's anvil, from Newstead (Roxburghshire) for clearing land or trade. [p. 132]

(*b*) The Multangular tower, York, of *c*. A.D. 300: the neater masonry is Roman, the larger Plantagenet. [p. 61]

PLAN OF EXISTING REMAINS

The London gate of Verulamium (restored). [p. 77]

4

Celtic fields, Smacam Down (Dorset) . *Crown Copyright* [p. 131]

Cameo of a British bear, South Shields (Co. Durham). [p. 162]

(a) Ladle handle, Capheaton (Northumberland), depicting an Empress. Mercury, god of trade, with a pack-man and shepherdess, the deities of corn and wine, sea and river – an epitome of British trade. [p. 198]

(b) Head of Claudius from Camulodunum, found in the 'River Alde (Suffolk): a relic of religion, loyalty, and revolt. [p. 108]

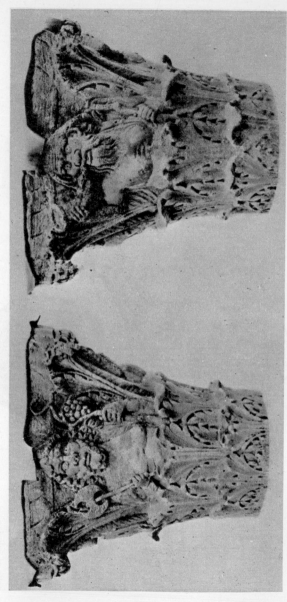

Capital from Corinium (Cirencester), with Autumn and Winter, in north-west European style. [p.190]

8

out some reference to those mosaic pavements which have so often indicated their existence. The most famous and most evocative are those decorated with figure-scenes from mythology. But when an attempt is made to estimate the position of the patron in the choice of pattern, it must be borne in mind that the range of patterns available will have depended upon the pattern-book of the firm which laid the pavement. Again, the execution of the work might vary sharply according to the competence of the worker. A striking example of this is furnished by the Cirencester pavement of the Four Seasons, of which, out of three surviving, two are fashioned with sensitive grace while the third is a coarse and clumsy rendering of the same subject, wholly lacking in deftness of line or subtlety of colour-blending. Entire compositions, based upon original designs of obvious breadth or delicacy, could become mere caricatures in the hands of inexperienced or over-ambitious workmen. Such are the Wolf and Twins pavement from Aldborough, now at Kirkstall Museum, Leeds, the Venus pavement at Rudston (E. Yorks), and the Apollo and Marsyas pavement, from Lenthay Green, Sherborne (Dorset). A comparable failure in detail marred the Horkstow pavements, though in some reproductions of lost examples the copyist must bear his share of the blame. The fact that such standards of workmanship passed muster serves as a check upon the sensibility of Romano-British patrons. It is clear that many were about as far from an appreciation of classical taste as a worker of samplers from a designer of Gobelins tapestry. What is remarkable is that they should have wanted such things at all, particularly when a rich and attractive variety of conventional patterns in abstract design was also available, which native instinct would have prompted them to choose. The choice then becomes something purposeful, as deliberate as Chaucer's choice of classical legend and interpreted in as crude an idiom. It becomes a reflection, however pale, of classical culture.

There is no doubt, then, that the richer villa-owners appreciated classical themes, and it is certain that many of their choices were directly linked with classical habits of mind or behaviour. The Dido pavement from Low Ham need not mean that its owner was an enthusiast for Vergil, but its existence does mean that this was the idiom of his choice; while the style of the design suggests that an African workshop may have produced the pattern. The Otford (Kent) wall-plaster, with its Vergilian scenes and quotations, attests that same feeling in a kindred field. No less striking are the dining-room pavements from Aldborough and Lullingstone. In the former house, the undecorated semicircular margin which, in the Roman manner, held the three couches for diners, looked on to a rich panel, now vanished, which formed a complementary centre-piece to the nine standing figures of the Muses with Greek inscription. In the latter villa a well-drawn and spirited scene of Europa and the bull forms the centre-piece and is embellished by a verse couplet which has the amateurish ring of impromptu production of the dining-table. These pavements and their planning reflect good cheer and good company in the Roman style: what was mannered in the first century A.D. had become manners in the fourth.

Some pavements are even more positive in their reflection of exotic feeling. The Brading (Isle of Wight) pavements, with their scenes from Eleusinian legend, their astrologer sage and Abraxas, the Gnostic deity, must represent not only a special order from a client, but a specially concentrated line of taste. The Orpheus pavements of Cirencester and the south-west are a Romano-

British speciality and belong to a moment when the tale had become a vehicle of both pagan and Christian teaching. Dionysiac legend also had its place, as at East Coker (Somerset), where the story of the divine birth may be recognized. The Labours of Hercules appear at Bramdean (Hampshire), the story of Cyparissus at Leicester. These echo not Vergil, but the hardly less beloved Ovid. Genre scenes are less common, and this in itself suggests a fairly rigid adherence to the pattern-book rather than the commissioned composition. But the hunting-scenes from Pitney, unfortunately only fragmentary, or the combined chariot and horse race at Horkstow, the *bigae et equi desultorii* of Roman aristocratic sports, must represent the special commission, as plainly related to the particular tastes of the client as the Gnostic pavement at Brading.

A half-way stage between the purely conventional pattern and the figured pavement is represented by the marine compositions of sea-creatures, fish, and shell-fish, or by the heads of Neptune, commonly though not exclusively associated with baths. These also are based upon Mediterranean models, but the idea is one so easily borrowed that it would be unfair to dub them representative of Mediterranean taste. They stand rather for a specialized pattern applied to a particular type of activity, namely, bathing. The purely conventional pattern, on the other hand, is linked with no special room or purpose, and its ubiquity proclaims it as the prime favourite of Romano-British taste, with both patron and worker. There is no doubt that, as Sir Thomas Kendrick has observed, it ministered to the native British predilection both for abstract pattern and for that equality of emphasis upon pattern and background which gave them an almost magical interchangeability. There were, too, certain shapes, and notably the pelta, which had

long been part of the repertory of Celtic art: and these
were now employed, always with an eye to background,
in new patterns of classical rigidity wherein colour played
the major part. This was a new movement in British art,
matched by the contemporary advances in enamel-work.
As the vehicle of unity in design, colour now took the
place of flow and the desired effect, rarely unachieved,
was of a glowing kaleidoscopic pattern controlled by its
rigidity of form but softened by the fact that, while major
patterns produced the over-all effect, the eye might
dwell with equal satisfaction on minor designs within the
major units. Further the colour scheme was seldom harsh
or clashing: in contrast with the hot contrasts of Mediterranean marbles it reflects the cool days and soft colours of
the British climate. The colours glow, but in rich restraint,
as in a page of the Lindisfarne gospels.

Excavation at such villas as Park Street and Lockleys
has revealed that Romanized buildings succeeded native
farms of a primitive kind, composed of groups of rectangular or circular huts. But it is also a well-known fact
that throughout the province many forms of this poorer
sort retained their form little altered through the centuries and in general hardly affected by the Roman world
around them. Evidence for this continuity of native habit
abounds in large areas throughout the island: Salisbury
Plain, the Dorset chalk-lands, parts of the North and
South Downs, the Fenland, the Long Mynd, and Upper
Wharfedale may be cited as typical regions of the kind.
It would, however, be wrong to suppose that this ubiquity
of native farms represents the existence of an anti-Roman
movement or the presence of a populace reluctant to
avail itself of better conditions: for excavation reveals
that the inhabitants of such places were as Romanized as
their means permitted them to be. Some other explana-

tion of the state of affairs is therefore required, and the
way thereto is cleared if it can be accepted that the
Romanized villa and the native farm started from the
same cultural level; for it then becomes necessary to suppose that the difference must lie in the social relationship
of their occupants. The social framework of the Celtic
tribe was explained by the Romans in terms of their own
institution of *patroni* and *clientes*. This was a relationship based upon social duty: in return for the protection
and personal support of a wealthy *patronus*, Roman
clientes bound themselves solemnly to further his interests and perform his requests. The expression was accordingly used by Roman writers to convey Celtic clan
relationship. But clan relationship also had an economic
foundation, expressed in tenancy and rent. The chieftain
and his principal followers lived upon their tenants'
rents, whether in produce or stock; and the payment of
such rents on large villa-estates, both in money and in
kind, is shown upon the Moselle valley reliefs, already
quoted as in other respects applicable to this side of the
Channel. If the difference between the Romanized villas
and the farms of primitive native style can be recognized
as corresponding to the social distinction obtaining within
the tribe between landowners and tenants, then its continuation may be explained by the freedom from interference which tribal custom enjoyed under Roman rule
so long as the terms laid down by the treaty of settlement
were observed.

This kind of relationship is the easier to recognize and
accept, now that an old-established interpretation of
native farm-sites is passing into oblivion. The thick
clusters of huts and storage-pits which go to make up the
native farm used regularly to be interpreted as a village,
since it was not then taken into account that these flimsy

or unstable structures had short lives and were frequently renewed or discarded. In such settlements a complete and undifferentiated plan of all the remains gives an altogether misleading picture of activity, since in fact only a few of the features were in use at any given moment. The 'village', which was so common a feature on maps of Roman Britain, turns out to be a farm of the primitive type already well established in the island long before Roman rule, and an essential part of tribal economy. The broad distinction is to be drawn no longer between villas and villages, but between landowners of substance and their tenants or their neighbour smallholders. Further, while it is possible to deduce from archaeology the broad distinction only, Celtic story and legend indicate that the relationship must have been one of great variety, closely related to custom and individual grants or services on the one hand and strictly defined by tribal law upon the other. It has been shown by Mr C. E. Stevens how an extremely primitive type of tribal law concerning land-inheritance became in the fourth century A.D. the subject of a classic case in the highest Roman court of appeal.

The equipment of this kind of farm in corn-growing country is worth specification. The farmhouse and accessory buildings form a group of huts either round or rectangular in plan. They are never large: an average cross-dimension of twenty feet would err on the high side. It has often been stated in the past that some were furnished with rude hypocausts, as if the inhabitants had borrowed central heating from the Roman world. But the alleged hypocausts do not occur in huts and are in fact corn-drying ovens; for the British farmer, as Pytheas had noted in the fourth century B.C., often gathered his corn green and threshed it under cover. This demands parching of the grain to make it keep. The plan of these kilns and their flues varied considerably, now bowl-shaped, now T-shaped, now H-shaped, and now forked. But the principle of construction was always the same, to create a fire whose hot gases passed through flues and heated gently a floor never itself in direct contact with the flame. Comparable installations, of much greater size and more complicated construction, are found in the Romanized villas. Once dried, the grain was stored in basket-lined pits. Both the pits and the corn-drying ovens needed frequent renewal, and a site occupied over a long period therefore yields them in bewildering multiplicity The area of the farm is usually enclosed by a ditch and bank, and its comparative spaciousness, demanded in part at least by the room required for the various installations and their renewal, is again deceptive as an indication of either the peopling of the establishment or its capacity in output.

If the general social relationship of villas to small-holdings is clear, there are, however, many points upon which information is wholly lacking. It is known that in the southern area of Roman Britain the great plough, with massive coulter, was widely distributed, from Essex to Hampshire and Gloucestershire. These implements, first introduced in the Belgic area of pre-Roman Britain, are of uncertain form, but it is clear that while primitive methods of traction would enable them to be used in the smallest size of Celtic fields, 100 feet square, convenience would choose the larger sizes of field, up to 400 feet. The villas which were associated with this newer kind of agriculture may therefore be expected to have had a field-system of somewhat larger scale. This, however, has not yet been identified in detail, although the air-photographs of certain Oxfordshire villas, like Ditchley and Little Milton, show clear traces of a new lay-out of field boundaries to a generous scale in the immediate vicinity of the farmhouse. On the other hand, it may be regarded as equally certain that not a few con-servative villa owners will have derived their wealth from customary tenants engaged in farming in the old style, and will therefore be in close touch, as are certain villas north of Winchester, with unchanged field-systems of the old type. How much there was of a new style in agricul-ture, and in what relationship it stood to the old, are thus questions which can be asked but which must for the time being remain unanswered. Still less has there been detected any trace of the Roman fashion of centuriated fields, systematically laid out in large standard rectangles enclosed by a grid of accommodation roads. Such systems might be expected to occur in the vicinity of the *coloniae* at Lindum (Lincoln) or Glevum (Gloucester), and Haverfield went so far as to indicate a parallel but non-rectangular system of roads west of Camulodunum (Colchester). But no unimpeachable example of cen-turiation has yet rewarded either the field-student or the air-photographer. It seems evident that in the British province Roman fields of the regular agrimensorial pat-tern were, to say the least, extremely rare, though their identification has proved a will o' the wisp to many antiquaries.

The rarity of application of the Roman system of field-planning is emphasized by the practice observable over many hundred thousands of acres in the Fenland. This vast alluvial basin, famous for the fertility of its crops, has in historic times always been so waterlogged as to require extensive and systematic drainage for its development. In more modern times the necessary combination of central authority and skill was not found until the seventeenth and later centuries; but the possibilities of the area did

not escape the Romans, whose interest in the exploitation
of marshland was sharpened by the value of such terrain
in the Mediterranean soil and climate. The Fens were
drained by a series of wide canals, the most notable being
the Cambridgeshire and Lincolnshire Car Dykes, the
latter over seventy miles long. In conjunction with the
rivers, which in many places followed different lines from
those of to-day, these canals served both for drainage and
for transport. As drains, they acted as catch-waters, trap-
ping the flow from the adjacent uplands and keeping it
out of the Fens; and they were also linked with a complicated series of minor cuts which drained the fens themselves. As canals, they linked the Fenland with the Witham
at Lincoln, the Witham in turn being linked by means of
the Fossdyke with the Trent. Access was thus obtained to
the Humber and the Ouse, so that, as Stukeley long ago
remarked, it was possible to proceed by inland water-
ways from the Fens to York. Stukeley further perceived
that the importance of this connexion lay in the opportunity which it offered for the transport of the Fenland
produce to military supply-depots.

The foundation of the system has been shown by excavation to belong to the later years of Nero; a date which
has an important bearing upon the original design of the
scheme and upon the origin of the labour force required
both for the canals or drains and for the subsequent
farming. At that time the Roman northern frontier was
based upon Lincoln, and there was no reason for basic
military supplies to proceed further. The construction of
the Fossdyke canal to the Trent may well be an addition
to the scheme, after the advance of the legionary base
from Lindum (Lincoln) to Eburacum (York) in A.D. 71.
As for the labour required to make them, the works are
situated in land immediately adjacent to the territory of

the Iceni, and their construction belongs to the period just after the revolt of A.D. 61, which the Iceni had led. There can be little doubt that the conquered rebels were condemned to labour at the new works and were thereafter drafted to the new agricultural reserve thus created, working it upon terms much more favourable to Rome than to themselves. It might, then, be thought that the Romans would have imposed here their own system of field-planning. But when the new fields and farms made possible by the drainage are scrutinized upon the vast mosaic of air-photographs by which the late Major Allen, the Fenland Research Committee, and Dr St Joseph have revealed them, it becomes clear that, while the canals and the main roads across the area bear the systematic imprint of the Roman engineer, the farms, fields, and lanes are no less characteristically native. The conclusion is inevitable that the natives, once planted upon the spot, were left to work the land in their ancestral fashion, virtually no attempt being made to convert them to Roman agricultural methods. Only the canal-side granaries indicate the stage at which the Roman tax-collector entered into possession of the giant's share of the produce, and that it was barged away to Roman depots.

The systematic excavation of a Fenland farm has yet to be undertaken, just as certain forms of Fenland fields or lazy-beds call for elucidation by the spade. But in another area the brilliant reconsideration by Professor Hawkes of the early but exquisitely precise excavations undertaken by General Pitt-Rivers in Cranborne Chase reveals both the farmsteads and the farmers' state of servitude. When the number of storage-pits in use at one time on such farms is compared with the number in use under free enterprise in pre-Roman farms on similar soil, it is calculated that under Roman rule the Cranborne

Chase farmers were deprived of something like three-fifths of the yield, very different from the reasonable rates of taxation of one-twelfth or one-tenth which applied in other parts of the Roman world. It is not thought that the folk of this area were rebellious; but the Belgae, who owned it, had been violently hostile to Rome and hard fighting had been required to conquer them. In these circumstances the terms of capitulation will not have been merciful, and there are numerous analogies in the Roman world for punishment of an obstinate resistance by the reduction of the hostile populace to serfdom. But at least the native agriculturalist was left to pursue his own methods in field and farm unchanged.

That drastic changes could, however, be introduced is shown by the treatment accorded to the area in the later third century A.D. At this time many of the agricultural villages were deserted, and important instances appear of field-systems obliterated by a new class of large and systematically planned enclosures for cattle. The adjacent downland is also bordered by new dykes, which, when mapped in relation to timber-bearing soils, reveal themselves as delimiting ranch-land in relation to forests. This is a notable instance of a deliberate change in the planned economic development of government-controlled land. Cattle-raising and sheep-farming were substituted for ploughing; and it is to be observed that herds and flocks were among the famous features of British provincial economy by the opening of the fourth century A.D., when their qualities are extolled. With the sheep and their wool was connected cloth-production. This manufacture was also earning a reputation for Britain in the Roman world at large. The establishment of a government weaving-mill at Venta, mentioned in the *Notitia Dignitatum* or list of government appointments, may well be connected, if remotely, with these changes; for the Venta in question, whose tribe is not specified, is certainly to be identified with Venta Belgarum (Winchester). The cloth would be for the Services.

If in southern Britain there is some evidence of expansion of pastoralism at the expense of agriculture, in northern Britain the process was probably reversed. There is little evidence for agriculture on any scale but the smallest in the north in pre-Roman days. Indeed, it is noteworthy how the decorators of prized artistic objects choose either horses or cattle as their theme, both in pre-Roman and Roman days, and how cauldrons, for seething meat, continue to be one of the principal manufactures of the area. These facts imply a Homeric type of society or, if this be thought too sophisticated, a state of civilization akin to that of the Irish Celtic sagas, in which wealth is reckoned not in broad acres but in heads of cattle. Many of the upland native farms of Cumberland and Westmorland plainly continued to reflect these conditions. If they have any field-system, it comprises a limited number of tiny paddocks or crofts, unequal to supporting a family through the year. Their wealth and support lay in the adjacent hill-pastures, with valley feeding for the winter. But most of the cattle, as in medieval times, must have been killed off when winter came, the most valuable arisings then being their hides and horns, convertible to leather and a variety of horn objects. The Roman tax-collector had a first interest in the herds, which were counted and taxed by heads: but his second and no less important interest lay in the hides. The consumption of hides by the Roman army must have been enormous. The jerkins and breeches of the soldiery, their shield-coverings and their tents, not to mention their massive boots, were all made of leather, and a tribute of hides will have been an obvious alternative to a tribute of corn. Thirdly, there was an interest in the carcass: for lard was also needed by the army in great quantity, as being, with corn and coarse wine, one of the staple articles of diet provided by the Roman government for its troops: and this too could be exacted from pastoral communities, whether cattle or pigs provided it.

One of the effects of the *pax Romana*, which stopped cattle-raiding between the different local groups, was to encourage an increase of population among the upland herdsmen of Westmorland and doubtless elsewhere. There came a time when the main settlements swarmed and minor farms grew up not far away, so that all the available land in the neighbourhood must have been pastured to the full. This is particularly evident in such a valley as that of the Lyvennet, south of Penrith, and other areas tell the same story. The increase did not necessarily spell prosperity for the individual: it may in fact have meant the reverse. But it did mean a rise in the amount of taxable property, when it came to counting animals, not to mention the possibilities of army recruitment.

There were, however, areas amid the fells and forests which show undeniable traces of a spreading agriculture. An outstanding example is Upper Wharfedale, where many miles of native field-systems exist, studded with native farms yielding Roman pottery and coins down to the close of the fourth century A.D. The Aire Gap was even opened to the villa system, though it must be significant that the single known example, at Gargrave in Craven, lies on the margin of an old glacial lake-bed, whose especially fertile land must have caught the eye of a wealthy man bent upon profitable farm-development. Similarly, the sole villa yet known in County Durham, at Old Durham, lies upon the magnesian limestone belt,

which still carries the best farming land in the area.
Whether these establishments belonged to native landowners or to Roman ex-soldier settlers must remain uncertain. But veteran settlers are known elsewhere in the
north and it would be wrong to suppose that all the land-
development was due to native enterprise. The fort of
Bremetennacum Veteranorum (Ribchester, Lancashire)
was the administrative centre of an enclave of veterans
important enough to figure in a Roman geographical
list. The Calder basin, from above Huddersfield to Castle-
ford, has yielded altars dedicated to the tutelary deity of
the Brigantes by Roman citizens whose names strongly
suggest that they too were veteran settlers. Nothing, however, is known of what form their settlements took or
what kind of production was connected with them. If
they were veterans then a land-settlement is most likely;
and it should be observed that the Middle Gritstone,
which the river Calder here cuts, supports good and
comparatively light agricultural land.

Wharfedale and its upper basin are intimately related
to an exceptional form of habitation, namely, the limestone cave-dwellings which are a feature of the Pennines
and Peak District wherever geological conditions permit
their existence. These dwellings have in the past been
variously interpreted, but nearly always through the eyes
of a civilized mentality which could conceive of them
only as a refuge and not as a permanent dwelling. This,
however, is not the view taken of them by peasant communities, to whom they offer the prospect of a residence
drier and more permanent than a hut, much warmer in
winter and cooler in summer. It is therefore not surprising that many of the caves, villages, and field-systems are
intimately connected and that there is no real distinction
to be drawn between the one and the other. They cer-

tainly do not represent the habitations of refugees from Roman rule, for most of them show a long continuity of habitation and they are not difficult either to find or to smoke out, as was the practice in Roman Africa when they were used by outlaws in this way. They represent rather the ready adaptation by man of advantageous accommodation provided by Nature: an extra possibility in housing as opposed to an emergency measure.

Lake-dwellings are another specialized form of settlement which owe their existence to human adaptation of a natural feature. These are little known in Britain south of Hadrian's Wall, though they had existed during the pre-Roman Iron Age in the Somersetshire marshes, as the famous examples at Glastonbury and Meare attest. But in certain parts of southern Scotland, notably Galloway and Upper Clydesdale, they are well known in both the first and second centuries A.D. Unfortunately, most of the excavations of these very interesting but complicated northern structures were conducted when archaeological technique was less equal to dealing with them than it is to-day, and a modern examination of an untouched site is highly desirable. They normally comprise artificial islands or platforms built on the edge of lakes and carrying substantial timber huts. Their special interest lies not merely in their structural details, but in the fact that their damp occupation layers frequently conserve intact perishable objects of wood, horn, and leather which the ordinary habitation site does not retain.

The varied scene of agricultural and pastoral activity provided by the numerous villas and farms demands for its completion the existence of markets and fairs: regional markets, held at comparatively frequent intervals, for the agricultural produce; fairs much less frequent and related to wider areas for the seasonal sales of animals. Within the canton, there might be several market-centres, and the cantonal capital need not necessarily have attracted the most important. The fairs might be so important as to attract folk from several cantons. But whenever or wherever they were held it is likely that in Britain, as throughout the ancient world, many were specifically associated with ancient sanctuaries whose deity hallowed the transaction and gave to the market or fairground a sacred peace which folk no less superstitious than quarrelsome would not violate by quarrels and brawls. The actual shrines where such gatherings may be detected are, however, few and detailed knowledge of them is still rare. Two may be cited, in widely separated districts.

The first is at Gosbecks Farm, three and a half miles south of Colchester, revealed by air-photography and since tested by excavation on a small scale. In its Roman guise, the place consisted of a temple of native pattern, the tall box-like shrine, with windows high above a veranda surrounding it, described in further detail below (p. 192). This building lay much off centre in a very large rectangle, bordered by a colonnaded enclosure, comprising two separate internal and external porticos, the internal designed to shelter worshippers, the external at the disposal of the general public. The planning indicates that, while the temple was undoubtedly important, other holy things, such as statues or venerated trees, occupied the sacred area; and that the area in question was an ancient pre-Roman holy place is demonstrated by the fact that the building had been substituted for an original large ditch, surrounding the same rectangular plot and containing pre-Roman rubbish. Outside the enclosure lay a great theatre, as at not a few sanctuaries in Roman Gaul, showing that crowds were expected and that their entertainment was catered for by stage per-

formances secular or religious – a distinction very much
more blurred in ancient times than now. As for deities,
the place has yielded a beautiful bronze statue of Mercury, the god of trade and commerce, with classic stance
but North-Gaulish features. The devotion to Mercury
leaves no reasonable doubt of the association of this
sanctuary with trade. The presence of large crowds suggests religious festivals combined with fairs or markets;
while the native character and ancestry of the sanctuary
dissociates it from the newly-introduced institutions of the
adjacent Roman colonia and attaches it to local habit and
tradition. It may be regarded as certain that Gosbecks
was the scene of well-frequented fairs or markets, and the
fact that it lay not far from the pre-Roman capital of the
Trinovantes may be thought to have enhanced its
importance.

The Gosbecks sanctuary was near a town. The second
site lies at Woodeaton, in the open country north-east of
Oxford, not far west of the half-way point along the
Roman road between Dorchester on Thames and Alchester. These were both minor cantonal centres, on the
borders of the Dobunni and Catuvellauni, and not certainly assignable to either. The nature of the place has
until very recently been doubtful, but it has long been
known for the very large amount of coins of small
denomination found there, ranging from the early days
of the province until the close of the fourth century A.D.
Indeed, there were a few authenticated records of still
later Roman coins, such as circulated during the fifth and
sixth centuries A.D., as if the spot had continued to be
frequented, as a remote centre in the backwoods very
well might. In addition to the coins there was a scatter of
small objects of votive character, such as miniature bronze
axes, small bronze birds, and crudely modelled plaques,

which strongly suggested the existence of a shrine. The suggestion has recently been proved correct. The spade has revealed, on the low ridge which carries the site and somewhat below its summit, a well-built temple of native type standing in an irregular straight-sided enclosure. As at Gosbecks, it might seem that the temple stood to one side of the most significant point on the site, in this case the summit; but there is no clue as to what, if anything, stood there and it can only be said that the highest point on the site was not included within the temple precinct. Nor is the deity or deities worshipped at Woodeaton known: among the votive objects a sort of duality can be detected, the axes suggesting a god with some characteristics at least of Mars, the birds a goddess. Celtic deities often went in pairs, and the cult objects, so far as they go, would suggest a pair like Sucellus and Nantosvelta, as opposed to Mercury and Rosmerta. Whoever they were, these deities attracted large crowds: and there is in addition a wealth of small objects that lie outside the range of offerings and suggest, no less strongly than the abundant small change, the existence of periodic fairs which thronged Woodeaton with buyers and sellers as well as worshippers.

In the north no such sites connected at once with commerce and religion are known to archaeology. But literature mentions the *Locus Maponi*, or meeting-place of Maponus, the Celtic god who was equated with the classical Apollo in his double aspect of youth and harper. This place may reasonably be identified with Clochmabenstane on the north shore of the Solway, where in later days the medieval English and Scottish wardens of the Marches met to settle common affairs. But the name is composite, half Brythonic and half English, *stane* having been added by Anglians who did not understand the

Brythonic *cloch*. So the stone of Maponus was a traditional meeting-place, and in Roman frontier politics
played its part as one of those permitted places of assembly
for markets and public business which enabled Rome to
control tribal gatherings. It is significant, too, that the
god under whose auspices the assemblage took place was
not a war-god, but a bardic god whose function was the
peaceful entertainment of music. Other *loca* there were,
but their names, where intelligible, are connected with
tribes and not with deities, unless indeed the tribes, like
the Brigantes, with their deity Brigans or Brigantia, had
a guardian god or goddess whose name was identical
with the adjectival form of their own.

Not all sanctuaries were connected with fairs and
markets and the number of shrines scattered through the
countryside must have been very large indeed. To describe them individually is quite outside the scope of this
volume, though some of the cults associated with them
are considered by themselves in another chapter. Here,
however, certain classes may be mentioned since they
must have formed one of the most characteristic features
in the rural landscape, quite apart from the cult of which
they formed the centre.

The most important is the pilgrim-sanctuary, of which
the shrine of Nodens at Lydney, on the north side of the
Severn estuary, provides a striking example. Nodens, who
was sometimes equated by his worshippers with Silvanus,
was certainly a god of hunting. But the bronze applied
decoration on one of the ritual crowns of his ministrants
shows that he was also a water-god, who journeyed
majestically over the waves in a car drawn by four sea-
horses: one thinks of the Severn bore, which begins near
Lydney its formidable sweep at every tide. His temple,
which belongs to after A.D. 364, occupies a prominent

Figure 11. Lydney, the late fourth-century pilgrim shrine
of Nodens

spur overlooking the estuary. It was a large building
divided into nave and ambulatory, the latter equipped in
due course with side-chapels. It was lavishly furnished
with mosaic pavements, the most important of which, in
the sanctuary, carried an inscribed dedication by the
chief of a naval repair-yard (*praefectus reliquationis*) and
his staff-interpreter. The plan of the building belongs to

neither the Celtic nor the purely classical world, but is a form borrowed from the East; and the suggestion has been made, without definite proof, that it owes something to Christian inspiration. The most interesting buildings, however, so far as the social side of the Lydney establishment is concerned, are those which surround the temple court, which occupies the whole of the hill-top. There is a long portico, rather like one side of a cloister, divided into open-fronted cells. This is a type of building well-known in classical sanctuaries of healing, where the sick slept in hope of divine counsel through dreams or even of personal curative action by the god or his priests. On an adjacent side to that occupied by the portico lay a courtyard building with numerous rooms and a large and imposing front reception-hall. A commodious set of Baths associated with this inn or guest-house add the essential hall-mark of Roman civilization. It is obvious that the establishment was planned for well-to-do visitors, who could pay good fees for attentions or benefits received. But not all the functions of Nodens were related to healing. As a god of hunting, he was expected by some of his worshippers to seek out and restore lost property, so that he was a god whose functions were hardly less diverse than his nature. Historically, the most interesting side of this cult is its late date, in an Empire slowly becoming Christian; and no less remarkable than this solidity of paganism is the fact that in the last quarter of the fourth century A.D. a site of this kind, overlooking the Bristol Channel, could be considered a safe and even lucrative proposition. The status of one of its important patrons as a naval officer is a pointed reminder of the fleet to which the district owed its peace and safety.

The temple of Nodens lies on a hill-top and within the lines of an ancient hill-fort. It was thus with another late-

Roman sanctuary, which was established, again after
A.D. 364, in the long-deserted but gloriously imposing
hill-fort of Maiden Castle, the ancient Dunum, which
had been superseded by the Romanized town of Durnonovaria in the seventies of the first centuries A.D. The
shrine built here was a simple edifice of the box-like
Celtic plan, though the deity worshipped therein was a
highly complicated being who combined with a human
nature those of an owl and a bull. Side by side with the
shrine lay a small priest's house. The furnishings of the
temple had been costly, and included imported marble,
but there is no hint here of accommodation for pilgrims
or the like, although the place was in fact much less
remote than Lydney from a civilized community. It may
well be asked what general notion prompted the late
establishment of sanctuaries in the old deserted high
places? There are other examples, as at Lydney, Chanc-
tonbury Ring (Sussex), and Harlow Hill (Essex), and it
can hardly be doubted that more existed. Was it the final
flicker of paganism, or a turning to the old gods in centres
of ancient valiance as times grew more uncertain? Or
were the ancient gods taking refuge in the wilderness as
Christianity spread in the towns? In some places, indeed,
the old gods remained firmly in possession of their pre-
Roman shrines. This state of affairs, already noted at
Gosbecks, is exemplified by Frilford, north-west of Abing-
don, where two Romanized shrines lie on top of an
earlier wooden building. This pre-existing building had
taken the form of a circular ditched enclosure containing
an open covered shed, like a *presepio*, where holy images,
cult objects, or offerings had been exposed to view. In the
Roman period this earlier shrine was razed to the ground
and replaced by a circular enclosure of which the contents are not now evident, while a new temple of the

native box-like form was built alongside and later received an extension. Occupation of this site continued into the fifth century A.D. and there can be no doubt either of the antiquity or the popularity of this country shrine or group of shrines. As a group, of which other members perhaps remain to be discovered, it resembles the forest sanctuaries of Roman Gaul, where numerous godlings attracted to a single holy spot their several groups or categories of worshippers.

Wayside shrines form another common class. These are the Surrey temples at Titsey on the Downs, adjacent to the Roman road between London and the Ouse valley, and the temple at Farley Heath, Albury. A different type is the shrine which yielded a relief of Diana and a hound, plainly a hunter's meeting-place, a pagan Chapelle de St Hubert, on the Fosse Way at Nettleton Scrub, ten miles north-east of Bath. The Watling Street shrines at Barkway (Hertfordshire), dedicated to Mars Alator, and Stony Stratford (Buckinghamshire), dedicated to Toutates, produced the beautiful silver plaques now in the British Museum, but no building which has been recorded. North of Lancaster, the shrine of Ialonus, god of the meadow-land, which again is known from an altar and not from buildings, lay close to the Roman road heading for the fort at Watercrook, near Kendal.

Spring and river-gods also had their sacred dwellings. At Chester-le-Street, Condatis, god of the watersmeet, had an altar at the confluence of the River Wear and the Cong Burn. Verbeia, goddess of the River Wharfe, was worshipped at Ilkley. No temple at the source of a great river is known in Britain, but it can hardly be doubted that they existed, particularly when rivers frequently bore divine names, such as Belisama (the Ribble), Deva (the Dee), or Brigantia (the Brent).

A hunter's shrine at Nettleton Scrub has already been mentioned. More romantic relics of ancient hunting are the shrines of Silvanus which sprang up in lonely cloughs on the high moors of the Pennines. These were erected by the commandants of Roman forts, wealthy men, mostly on the first rungs of their careers in the Imperial Civil Service, to commemorate successful hunting expeditions. Two are attested by altars only; one stone dedicated by Aurelius Quirinus, commandant at Lanchester (Co. Durham) and found at Eastgate in Weardale; the other erected by Sabinianus, commandant of a cavalry regiment, in remote Bollihope, 'after catching a lovely boar which previous hunters had hunted in vain'. The third boasts both altars and shrines: it lay higher still, on the Eller Beck, south of Bowes (Yorkshire), 1275 feet above sea-level. There the local commandant, Caesius Frontinus, and one of his centurions set up separate shrines to Vinotonus, a stream-god whom the centurion identified with Silvanus. The temples were simple structures, one round and the other rectangular, with stone walls and thatched roofs. Their ruins still half buried the altars when they were first observed by a shepherd. If this could happen after seventeen centuries, how manifestly grim and true must have been the allusion of Gildas in the sixth century A.D. to the ruins of shrines everywhere, 'their walls, inside and out, bristling with weathered idols of savage mien'. His phrase reveals in startling fashion the effect of belief in a multiplicity of deities upon the landscape of the countryside when the power of heathendom was exalted.

Sacred groves are archaeologically unresponsive, though the planning of many temple enclosures seems to imply their existence. But place-names in Britain indicate a very few of the many there must have been. The Celtic word for such a spot was *nemeton*, which is explained in an ancient glossary as meaning, in the plural, *sacra silvarum*, 'the holy places of the woods'. It occurs in Cornwall or south-west Devon in the name Nemetotatio, in Monmouthshire in the form (Ne)metambala, and in Derbyshire as Aquae Arnemctiae, the name for Buxton, in which the second element applies to the goddess dwelling 'over against the *nemeton*'. The Buxton grove no doubt overshadowed the source of the healing waters. A little further south, on the Fosse Way in Nottinghamshire, Vernemeton, means 'the great grove' according to the Gaulish bishop Venantius Fortunatus. Finally, in Scotland, not far from the Antonine Wall, there is Medionemeton 'middle grove' or 'mid-way grove', which has been identified, attractively but not with complete certainty, with the prehistoric sanctuary at Cairnpapple (West Lothian).

Lastly, there are the tombs and cemeteries. Folk in Britain had for long ages been used to great tombs as features of the landscape. The habit of according prominent positions to barrows of the Bronze and Iron Ages ensured that few sky-lines were without these arresting land-marks. The outsize in all barrows, Silbury Hill, formed the sighting point for the Roman road from Mildenhall (Wiltshire) to Bath. It should, however, be remembered that the habit of building these circular tumuli continued into Roman times, and that Roman roads in certain parts of Britain, as in the Meuse basin in north-eastern Gaul, were frequently lined with them. The Six Hills at Stevenage are a famous group, by the side of the western loop of Ermine Street. The road from Salisbury to Dorchester is flanked by three at Badbury Rings. But these last are outliers. The great concentration is in East Anglia, where these barrows certainly

carry on the traditions of an Iron-Age aristocracy, whose
rich tumuli, opulently furnished with imports from the
Roman world, are so notable a feature of the area in the
first half of the first century A.D. For these people, however, it was the internal content of the tomb and luxurious objects buried with the dead which counted as
important. From the Roman point of view the external
aspect of the monument was also highly significant; not
for sombre grandiosity, which characterizes the monuments of the Republic, nor for religious symbolic ornament, associated with tombs of the later Empire, but for
relief sculpture intended to give a lasting picture or
memorial of the daily life and advocations of the deceased,
as it were a record of their very being. In Gaul such
monuments, which took their form from the Mediterranean world, occasionally survive almost intact, like the
famous example at Igel, in the Moselle valley. On this
the daily life, and, less prominently, the work, of a rich
family engaged in cloth-production covers the panels and
friezes of a lofty and slender monument crowned by a
very high and concave roof, almost like a crocket; and
mixed with these secular representations are the myths
of Hercules, typifying the religious beliefs of the family
as well. Britain retains no such monument. But it must be
recalled that knowledge of the majority of those in Gaul
is derived from the use of their sculptured blocks and
slabs in the foundations of late-Roman walls. The only
walls in Britain which have as yet yielded materials of
this kind in abundance are the London bastions and the
Constantian north wall of Chester. The former happen
to have yielded early monuments only, the great altar
tomb of the procurator Classicianus, and soldiers' monuments from near the fort of the standing garrison. The
latter produced a variety of material from a most inter-

esting series of small monuments but nothing on the grand scale, for vast and costly tombs could hardly be expected outside a legionary fortress. It would, however, be rash to suppose that monuments of the Igel scale never existed in southern Britain. The foundations of an elaborate circular tomb occupying the middle of a small cemetery at Harpenden (Hertfordshire), reveal it to be of the monumental class, with central, niched tomb-chamber containing at least one life-sized statue. It had angle-pilasters, implying a decorative treatment of the front with the round tower-like structure rising above. Another very large tomb was the circular mausoleum at West Mersea (Essex), a stone-revetted structure with earth fill, sixty-five feet in diameter, braced by radiating walls and marginal buttresses. A circular mausoleum, thirty feet in diameter, with external buttresses, occurs at Keston (Kent) in association with a villa. Certain country districts have also yielded walled cemeteries. That at Harpenden (Hertfordshire), already noted, was walled. But Kent boasts of six at least, among which Lockham contained two monumental tombs, Plaxtol a barrow, Sittingbourne a monumental tomb, and Springhead, near Southfleet, some very rich finds, including elaborate shoes of purple leather ornamented with gold thread. The reason why such monuments do not survive in Britain is to be sought in their distribution, which covers the south-eastern districts of the island that are devoid of good building-stone. Folk of later ages have seized upon the Roman stonework with avidity.

Roman triumphal monuments in the open countryside would be rare. But the foundations of a famous one exist at Rutupiae (Richborough), the principal port of entry to the province. They form an enormous base 30 feet deep below ground level, 145 feet long and 105 fee

wide, including a flange for a few steps. The structure
which was thus carried was cased in Carrara marble and
its main columns were not less than 50 feet high. There
may well have been a second stage above this and there
were certainly some massive bronze statues, of which
small fragments have been found. The monument was
built about A.D. 100 and may have commemorated
Trajan's settlement of the province. It is comparable with
the Tetrapylon or four-way arch erected at the two main
entrances to the province of Egypt in honour of Claudius,
and this may well have been the actual form of the monument. Later, towards the close of the third century A.D.,
it was stripped of its ornaments and served as a fortified
look-out post against Saxon pirates, a choice no doubt
determined by its great height.

No other monument of the kind can be tied to a specific
site. But inscribed blocks from a monument commemorating the erection of Hadrian's Wall were used in building the Saxon monastery church at Jarrow (Co. Durham). An Italian marble head of provincial style found
at Hawkshaw, in the wilds of the Upper Tweed basin, is
more problematic. It cannot have come from far away,
its Roman date is not in doubt and its occurrence is perhaps least difficult to explain by connecting it with a
triumphal monument; of which, however, no structural
remains have been identified.

CHAPTER FOUR

ECONOMICS

WHEN the geographer Strabo, writing early in the principate of Tiberius (A.D. 14–38), but recording many things of a generation or two earlier, gives an account of British exports to the Continent, he reflects conditions in south-eastern Britain and particularly the exports at the disposal of tribal chiefs and their followers. Corn, cattle, hides, and hunting-dogs attest the agriculture and stock-raising of Sussex, Kent, and Essex. Slaves represent the profit of raiding expeditions on the fringe of these areas. The metals, however, must have come from further afield: silver from the Mendip or Peak lead deposits; tin from Cornwall, gold from Wales, and iron from Wales or the Weald. The trade in metals implies, in fact, as in pre-historic days, particular connexions more widely developed. The statement concerning metals reverses, too, the hasty conclusion of Cicero, derived from his brother on Caesar's staff, that there was in Britain 'not so much as a scruple of silver'.

Metals in any province were almost exclusively State property, and formed an important item in the provincial budget. In Britain, the principal metal product was lead, which sounds dull, until it is recalled that the only way of producing silver known to the ancient world was by cupellation from lead, and that the abundant British lead represents a by-product from silver extraction. In the Roman world silver was the most regular money of account, and the need for large quantities explains the rapid development of British lead resources, attested by the numerous date-stamped ingots, or pigs, of the metal. The Mendip mines were in production by A.D. 49, six years after the conquest, the Flintshire mines by A.D. 74, the mines of Nidderdale, Yorkshire, by A.D. 81. All these dated pigs, and most others, are from direct Imperial working, but some undated examples from Derbyshire, and one early but undated example from Flintshire, bear the stamps of lessees, all Roman mercantile citizens. Rarer still, but again associated with the Derbyshire area, are the pigs of the Lutudarum Company (*socii Lutudarenses*) which took its name from the principal centre in the mining district, perhaps Chesterfield, and traded its pigs in large numbers by water to the Humber. The quantity of lead extracted from Britain was very large and the Romans were struck by the ease with which it could be mined. The elder Pliny refers to much opencast mining. But he adds a significant and curious fact, that production was restricted, in favour of the Spanish market. This is one of the rare cases in which such artificial controls are known to have been applied, though similar action was taken in relation to the vine-growing in Gaul.

Of working and organization very little is known. In the Mendips the principal centre was Charterhouse on Mendip, where the remains of a mining settlement cover a considerable area and are graced by a small amphitheatre. An early pig from this area is countermarked by the Second Legion and this might suggest soldiers in charge of convict labour, for relegation to the mines was in the Roman world a form of penal servitude. But no evidence exists either way in the Mendips for the continuity of this practice, if it was in fact there applied. The Imperial stamped ignots continue until A.D. 164–9, though some are countersigned with private company's marks, while another carries the name of C. Nipius

Ascanius, a Roman citizen lessee who is also known in Flintshire. After that they appear no more, and it may well be that the working of the mines was then delegated to the *curiales* or tribal council, or to private concessionaires. This at least became the practice in other important Roman mining areas. If so, it would certainly account for the abundance of late-Roman silver coinage in the Somersetshire area, since the *curiales* would be receiving a substantial percentage of the output, returned to them in the form of silver coinage. In the fourth century A.D. Britain was still famous for its metal output, and the quantity of pewter and lead objects belonging to the period bears witness to its copiousness.

In the earlier period of Imperial working there is some evidence for the export of Mendip lead. The pig countermarked by the Second Legion was found at St Valery-sur-Somme, while one occurs at Stockbridge (Hampshire) and two on the Solent. This suggests a traffic of consignments across the Channel and along the main arterial route to Southern Gaul or Italy. It is not likely, however, as the administrative fragmentation of the Empire developed, that this traffic continued brisk.

The earliest stamped pig associated with Flintshire is of A.D. 74; and, if the annexation of the area occurred in A.D. 61, there would be evidence for rapid exploitation, as in the Mendips. The Italian concessionaire, C. Nipius Ascanius, cannot be much later, since his countermark appears on a Mendip pig of A.D. 59. The centre of the actual mining seems to have been Halkyn Mountain, as to-day, while the mining settlement lay at Pentre Ffwrndan, one mile south-east of Flint, where pottery and coins suggest an occupation beginning about A.D. 70 and continuing until at least the close of the second century A.D. There is also some evidence, though it is not strong,

for third-century exploitation at Meliden, at the northern tip of the Clwydian mountains, in the Talar Goch
mine. It would be interesting to know whether this was
the reason for the foundation of the adjacent military
site, at Prestatyn, on a then navigable coastal creek. The
pigs from the Flintshire area are stamped *Deceangl*,
for *metallum Deceanglicum*, the name surviving in the
medieval district of Tegeingl and to-day in a deanery.
This was the name of the tribe which the manuscript of
Tacitus presents as Decangi, the metropolitan version of
a name which must have seemed oddly barbaric to a
Latin ear.

The next dated group of lead pigs is the small group
from Yorkshire, which also carry the tribal name of the
area, in the form *Brig*, for *metallum Briganticum*. They
are found in the area between Nidderdale and Wharfedale, which was much exploited in later medieval times
for lead also. The earliest dated example is of A.D. 81,
exactly ten years after the Roman acquisition of the area.
Another, of Trajan (A.D. 98–117), is imperfectly recorded
from Pateley Bridge. It is probable that this was not the
only lead-bearing area worked in Yorkshire. There is a
good local tradition of Roman exploitation of the Swale-
dale lead deposits, in particular the Hurst Mine; it is
connected with a pig of Hadrian, unfortunately never
recorded in detail.

The Derbyshire lead field is one of the largest and most
productive in Britain. There is evidence for Imperial
working under Hadrian, but in addition many undated
pigs are stamped with the names of private lessees. The
fact that these names have a first-century ring about them
does not definitely exclude a later date. The Roman
name of the field, or its centre, was Lutudarum and
appears also as qualifying the name of a private com-

pany, the *socii Lutudarenses*. At what stage, however, the *socii* occur or in what order they came in relation either to the individual lessees or the Imperial working, or whether, again, all or any two were contemporary, is quite unknown. It may be observed, however, that the *socii* sent down their pigs in large numbers to Petuaria (Brough on Humber), either to their own warehouse or to local wholesalers. Yet another aspect of exploitation is the lead ore from stream deposits found in the Roman fort at Navio (Brough on Noe), from which the district was in part policed. This implies a system of collection by natives for which the fort served as central depot. The whole picture in Derbyshire is thus a complicated one. The relationship of the various elements is obscure; the administrative centre of the field is not fixed, though it is named, and the duration of the exploitation is unknown. This makes the record tantalizing and leaves only an abiding impression of intensive activity in an area attractive to the Imperial agent and the commercial speculator alike. Hadrianic working of lead is also attested in south-west Shropshire, in the Shelve and Snailbeach areas. Here the Twentieth Legion took some hand in supervision or organization of the mining, since it counter-marked at least one pig, found at Châlon-sur-Saône and dated to A.D. 195. Beyond this, however, there is no evidence for later Imperial working, and it may be that the field was turned over to concessionaires or small lessees. It is, on the other hand, likely that the smaller field to the west, on the eastern slopes of Plynlimon, which was under development during the second century A.D., was always worked by the military. A road, as at Caermote (Cumberland), leads directly towards it from the fort of Caersws.

Military supervision was certainly exercised in the Alston lead-mines of south-west Northumberland, which were worked upon a smaller scale in the third century A.D. under the Second Cohort of Nervii. The stamped seals from consignments which reached Brough under Stainmore bear the name of the cohort and the legend '*metal(lum)*'. It is likely that some of the produce also went north-eastwards to Corstopitum (Corbridge), where some of the mineral wax associated with the Alston veins has been found. Yet another lead-mining settlement associated with the military is Machen in Glamorganshire, where slight remains of the village and some remains of the workings have been observed. It need hardly be doubted that in the military areas there were other ventures of the kind, since it became the policy of the Imperial government to develop local resources wherever possible. The pawky request of Nero's legionaries that 'commanders looking for silver should get their decorations in advance' would indeed have been out of date.

If the exploitation of lead may be regarded as of great importance both in itself and in relation to silver extraction, the copper workings of Britain were also of substantial value in themselves and in their relation to bronze, an alloy used in the Roman world for almost every hard-wearing purpose. The principal deposits of this metal lay in the north-west, in northern Shropshire, Caernarvonshire, and Anglesey. The Shropshire deposit is centred at Llanymynech, where the cave from which the veins have been worked by galleries was apparently inhabited by the miners.

Similar conditions appear to have existed in the Caernarvonshire copper mines of Great Orme's Head, where inhabited caves have also been noted, and associated objects date the activity to the third and fourth centuries A.D. This cave dwelling again suggests labourers tied to the spot, whether they were slaves or convicts, but it seems that no smelting was done on the spot, the ore being carried away for treatment elsewhere. The copper cakes found in Caernarvonshire are stamped with the names of at least two private companies; and this would support exploitation by slave labour, though it is not necessarily true for every mine or for every period. In Anglesey the picture is rather different. Here the principal mining area was Parys Mountain near Amlwch, though other activity is known, as at Aberffraw and Pengarnedd. But the copper cakes in the island are all associated with native villages, as if the ore were gathered by native labour and smelted piecemeal in the villages for eventual collection at a central depot. This would imply that the island, once the cult centre of the Druids, was treated as a temple estate with a fixed tribute transferred from the Druidical community to the Roman State. The mines will explain the continuing interest of the Romans in the fort at Caernarvon (Segontium) and their provision of naval stations both there and at Holyhead in order to protect the valuable raw material and its workers from pirates, or slave-raiders. It is significant that while there is no evidence for legionary occupation at Chester after A.D. 367, the Caernarvon fort was then re-occupied intensively, the occupation lasting until A.D. 383. Its cessation is connected in Welsh legend with not only the usurpation but the actual person of Magnus Maximus, in the guise of Maxen Wledig. Whatever the truth of the story, it at least coincides with the archaeological facts and with the economic value of the copper deposits. It should be emphasized that these are the most northerly and the most important copper deposits exploited by the Romans in Britain. The Cheshire mines at Alderley Edge do not appear to have been worked in Roman times, though well known to prehistoric and medieval man. The Yorkshire deposits at Middleton Tyas were too deep and too waterlogged and were only accessible after the advent of steam pumping-machinery.

Much the most famed of British metals in the days before the Roman occupation was tin. The vivid accounts by Diodorus Siculus, of overland pack-horse transport of Cornish tin from the Gallic coast to Narbo (Narbonne) in the first century B.C., and of the island emporium on the British coast, from which merchants obtained it, all speak of a brisk and flourishing early trade, monopolized in Caesar's day by the Veneti of Brittany. But in the Augustan age, when the conquest of north-western Spain made the Spanish tin deposits available, commercial interest in British tin ceased, while the anti-Roman refugee warriors from Gaul who were crowding into south-west Britain cannot have encouraged adventurers. Even when the island became a province and the Dumnonii one of the philo-Roman allied communities, it does not appear that the Roman government took much interest in developing the tin. There is slight evidence for activity in the first century A.D.: somewhat later the best evidence is the occurrence of two *stationes*, or Treasury Offices, in the area, presumably connected with the working or leasing of stanneries. The source which mentions them used for Britain material of the second century A.D. But only in the third century A.D., and particularly after the ruin of the Spanish mines in its last quarter, does Government interest in the area begin. Milestones from Gordian III (A.D. 244–9) onwards, with a special outburst of activity under Constantine and his house, attest new efforts in development. It is significant that now commences a very wide distribution of pewter table services; later in the century blocks of pewter with official stamps from the Thames at Battersea attest cargoes of this valuable metal being concentrated in London, the seat of the provincial Treasury administration. How late the development continued is not known. But it is a remarkable fact that in the sixth century A.D. a storm-blown Byzantine ship could unload its corn and relieve a famine in Exeter and return with a cargo of tin, as if the merchant adventurers of prehistoric days were repeating their experiences in the Dark Ages.

After tin came gold. Only one gold mine of the Roman age is known in Britain, at Dolau Cothi, near Pumpsaint, between Llanio and Llandovery, in north-east Caermarthenshire, among the Demetae. Here the workings are both open-cast and by long and deep adits, following the veins of gold-bearing pyrites. The adit galleries are very systematically cut, to serve for both drainage and haulage, and in the levels below them wheels for lifting water were installed to drain them, as in the Spanish mines. A panning cradle has also been found. At the shaft-head the ore was pounded, milled, and washed, a good head of water for the latter purpose being brought in a special aqueduct or open lade some eight miles long. A bath-house is also known, reminiscent of the bath-house at Aljustrel, mentioned in the Spanish *lex metalli Vipascensis.* The date of working is not defined, though some gold jewellery made on the spot is of late second- or early third-century style. The scale of working certainly attests either Government activity or a concessionaire company of high standing and efficiency. A detailed study of this most interesting scene of specialized Roman development is overdue.

The iron mines of Britain were numerous and hardly less productive than the lead mines. This was not accounted a valuable metal nor was its output restricted, for it is clear that there was always a good market for so useful a commodity. The principal deposits exploited by Rome lay in the Weald and the Forest of Dean. The former was being rapidly developed under Claudius and Nero by the native client-king Cogidumnus at Chichester, with a gild of iron-workers organized in Roman fashion. It is tempting to think that this represents the Romanization of a group of native smiths, who must already have had a special position in prehistoric economy. How the deposits were exploited when the native kingdom passed out of existence is unknown, but coins and pottery from many sites cover the whole Roman period. Very large quantities of slag and cinders were available for local road construction; and this might suggest that the *curiales* continued to develop the deposits in succession to the native king, using its by-product for road-making which was also a communal concern. Direct interest of the provincial government in some at least of the iron-workings is, however, suggested by the occurrence of the official stamped roofing-tiles of the *Classis Britannica*, or Fleet in Britain, in connexion with slag near Wadhurst (Sussex). No administrative or working centre for the Weald is known. In the Forest of Dean, however, much working was concentrated at Weston-under-Penyard (Ariconium), where earlier antiquaries noted an area of 200 acres covered with slag-heaps. Here exploitation can hardly have developed until after the conquest of the Silures in A.D. 74–6: the coins indicate activity from the late first century A.D. until the fourth, with a marked increase towards the end.

Further north, the iron-stones of Northamptonshire and Lincolnshire were also actively developed. There are large slag deposits and workshops, almost unexplored, at Clipsham; while a Roman blast-furnace has been noted at Woolsthorpe near Colsterworth and good evidence for working deposits in the vicinity of Scunthorpe. In York-shire, large heaps of clinker at West Bierley, near Cleck-heaton, were noted in the eighteenth century in associa-tion with coins of the late third and early fourth cen-turies A.D. Further north still, the military workshops at Corbridge, active in the third and fourth centuries A.D., were using iron ore brought into Corbridge as low-grade smeltings from native hearths. These blooms were then re-smelted in puddling furnaces for ultimate forging into weapons, nails, and hold-fasts produced in the workshops. The source of the material was undoubtedly the Redes-dale deposits, just south of the fort of Habitancum (Ris-ingham); and it was used again on Tyneside much later for Armstrong's early munition works. This picture of a military arsenal at work is one which is at present unique in the Roman world.

Coal was also mined in Roman Britain, though it never became, as far as is known, an item of export: and British coal is only mentioned once in Roman literature, as a curiosity to be seen upon the altars of Sul Minerva at Aquae Sulis (Bath). Its tendency 'to become round stone masses' will be noted with a smile. This was undoubtedly the Somersetshire cannel coal. But the Nottinghamshire coal has been noted in the Fenland villages. Local coals, microscopically identical with local veins, have been noted on Hadrian's Wall at Benwell, in a smithy, at Housesteads, and at Corbridge: and their use is dated to the second century A.D. at the first and last places and to the fourth century A.D. at the last two. It was also used in the second century A.D. on the Antonine Wall, at Castle-cary and Bar Hill forts; while less detailed observations attest coal in Roman forts at Risingham, South Shields, and Manchester. In industry coal was used for smelting lead at Pentre Ffwrndan, iron and glass at Wilderspool,

and iron at Weston-under-Penyard, and for heating hypocausts at Wroxeter and Caerwent. It must, however, be
recognized that wood or charcoal were the fuels much
more normally employed and that coal was used only
where it was handier to get than wood. In the Fenland,
to quote an extreme case, it would arrive as ballast in the
barges and be transported much more easily in the canal
system than logs.

Three other natural deposits provided not fuel, but
ornaments. The Kimmeridge shale of the Isle of Purbeck,
in Dorset, was worked extensively into jewellery,
decorative panels, and furniture. The personal decorations consist principally of lathe-turned bracelets, from
which the cores were so numerous as to win the name of
'Kimmeridge money'. But the material could also be cut
and carved in sheets, forming panels after the fashion of
marble veneering, or, when lightly hollowed, flat dishes
or trays. These table furnishings were modelled upon
metal prototypes, just as were Victorian trays of papier-
mâché, though the hardness of the shale suited the treatment better. Even furniture was thus made, table-legs
with claw-feet and sea-horse or sea-lion shoulders being
known and widely distributed in southern Britain, though
not common. Furniture of this kind must have been difficult and hazardous to manufacture, and consequently
both expensive to buy and frail to maintain, though it
could be kept in good condition by oiling. It should be
observed, however, that whenever this material is decora-
tively carved, its patterns run upon very strictly classical
lines, as if the firm operating the concession was Roman
in its emphasis, not to hazard a guess at its origin. A
detailed study of this very interesting Romano-British
industry is wanting.

The second natural deposit is Purbeck marble. This

was much used for mortars in which a very hard grinding or pounding surface was required, and vessels of this description are found very widely distributed over the province though more thickly near the source. It was also used to make tablets for important inscriptions, as far afield as Noviomagus (Chichester), Corinium (Cirencester), Verulamium (St Albans), Camulodunum (Colchester), Londinium (London), and Deva (Chester). The variety favoured was greyish-white in colour, and formed a particularly handsome speckled background to the vermilion lettering in cinnabar (*minium*) favoured in Roman monumental inscriptions. Panels and mouldings for decoration are well known and widely distributed, both in town and country, also lavers for public baths, as at Calleva (Silchester).

The third natural deposit is jet, associated with the Whitby lias, wherein it is found as lumps. Solinus describes British jet with interest, as a substance heated with water but quenched with oil and magnetic when rubbed. These paradoxical qualities endowed jet with almost magical esteem, and it became a favourite material for ornamental jewellery, much of which was manufactured at Eburacum (York). Hair-pins, spindles, finger-rings, and bracelets were made in great variety, some bracelets and many necklaces being ingeniously articulated in minute component pieces. Elaborately carved pendants and medallions, including family groups executed to order, and teddy-bears, represent other profitable lines of production. Whether the jet articles found in considerable profusion in the Rhineland represent imports from Britain or local working of the British raw material it is difficult to estimate: but it can at least be said that there are few Rhenish products which cannot be matched in Britain. It is also true that, as in the objects of Kimmeridge shale, the artistic tone of all these productions, British or Rhenish, is essentially Roman, and that native motifs are wholly absent. This Roman jet-working differs in finish from the modern Victorian, in not introducing a high polish: the effect is rather of restrained burnishing, certainly more attractive to sensitive taste.

Other natural products for which Britain won a modest fame were jewels. British pearls were of some repute, though their duskiness was deprecated. They were found both in rivers and on the sea-shore and were apparently not gathered from living oysters. Scottish rivers, in particular the Dee, are since known to have produced large examples. Amethysts were also won from an island in the Western ocean, and an island yielding gems is once mentioned in geography. The trade in hunting-dogs also continued, and three breeds at least are known in literature: the Irish wolf-hound, seven of which caused a stir in Rome when Symmachus exhibited them; the bull-dog, known to Claudian, and a small spaniel described in some detail by Oppian. The favourite dogs of the Castor ware potters, however, are of greyhound breed, like Diana's dog at Nettleton Scrub, and this would indicate a fourth variety. Bears were also exported, mostly for the arena, where they were already under Domitian used for lacerating criminals. In the fourth century A.D., when Claudian seeks a characteristic dress for a personification of north Britain, he gives her a bear-skin. If he had chosen a seal-skin the conception would have been equally apt, for the pelts of these creatures, in which Britain abounded, were both highly prized and highly priced in the Roman world. Furs and skins must have formed an important export.

Such British cloth as was famous abroad was probably of a special kind: the *birrus Britannicus* of Diocletian's price-list was a rain-cloak, and glossaries say that the cloth for such mantles was of goats' wool. But on the home market of the province there was certainly much sheeps' wool available; the fourth-century panegyrist praises the flocks laden with fleeces, and there can be no doubt that numerous villas were engaged in the various ancillary processes of wool production: fulling at Chedworth and Titsey, and, on an even larger scale, at Darenth, have already been mentioned. There should be added the fine pair of cropping-shears from Great Chesterford, now at Cambridge, which can only have come from a woollen-mill, though their function, to give the piece a firm nap, has now for long been performed by machinery. At Silchester a small dye-works was excavated, though its date within the Roman period remains uncertain. Linen is nowhere specifically mentioned, but its use on a large scale for finely-woven shrouds in the York district should be noted.

Food-stuffs are not recorded as regularly exported. But corn-export in A.D. 361 to the Rhineland is shown by the context as not an emergency measure. Oysters also, though not unknown to Italian epicures of the first century A.D., can hardly have travelled in quantity, and some senators at least must have tasted them in Britain itself. They formed, however, a very large trade within the province. Few Roman sites are without them and it is clear that in the taverns and shops outside the fortresses and forts of the province the oyster-bar was the Romano-British equivalent of the modern fried-fish shop. Mussels are on many sites almost equally numerous, and were no doubt cheaper, if less luscious.

Among British home industries, the best known, even though much more awaits discovery, are the potteries. The most renowned are those at Durobrivae (Castor on

Nene), excavated in desultory fashion in the nineteenth century by Artis and not since then seriously studied. These potteries turned out a great variety of vessels, though drinking-cups form the principal item. They are somewhat coarser in proportion than the Rhenish wares; the clay of which they are made fires to a lighter colour, and their finish is less brilliant or glossy. Their decoration in barbotine, is, on the other hand, of perhaps greater variety: the favourite conventional pattern is a running scroll of ivy-leaves, no doubt borrowed from contemporary plainer forms of Samian ware, but normally executed with a sweeping surety of touch which the more rigid Samian lacks. Very common, and animated by the same fresh and rapid handiwork, are the so-called Hunt cups, in which swift dogs chase hares or deer. Human scenes include chariot-races, gladiatorial combats, and, occasionally, scenes from classical mythology, while sometimes the place of humans or animals is taken by phallic emblems of good luck. The human scenes are seldom successful by classical standards. The very nature of the barbotine technique, by which the figures were traced in wet clay like icing sugar, made it impossible to catch the subtleties of the human form and denied to the artist the control of outline obtainable by incised technique or by carefully prepared moulds. It would have been wiser to be less ambitious, yet the ambition is of a kind which occurs in no other province. It is British in character, as stubbornly determined as the imitations of Chinese wares in a later age; and perhaps the most interesting side of the attempt is that this development should have been thought necessary to attract a market. It reflects, socially speaking, a purchasing public gladdened by hunting, racing, and stories of divine adventures. But while there is a vivid appeal to the imagination, there is no appeal to literacy. No attempt was made to imitate the inscribed wares of Rhenish manufacture. Further, the figured wares, to-day attracting most attention, formed in fact only a small part of the output. There was a large series of drinking cups, wholly undecorated or at most provided with scales on shoulder and side, to prevent the vessel from slipping in the hand. In addition there were elaborately rouletted round containers with lids, perhaps used for butter, cheese, or honey. The date of the output is not defined in detail on the site: but finds elsewhere show that it began well before the close of the second century A.D., and it certainly continued well into the fourth, though the figured vessels do not outlast the third century A.D.

The New Forest pottery is another and more restrained manufacture, whose period of production lasted from the later third century A.D. until the last quarter of the fourth. To judge from the types, the period of greatest output was in the first half of the fourth century A.D. This ware differs greatly from Castor ware. Its range of forms is much wider: flagons, dishes, bowls for table and kitchen, jars, cooking-pots, vases, goblets, and even candlesticks, appear in great quantity and certainly swamp the drinking-cups, though these also abound. Decoration, so far as it occurs at all, is restricted to very simplified running scrolls or conventional triangular patterns, all in white slip, and to repetitive stamped rosettes, demi-rosettes, or ogees. If Castor ware be thought the British counterpart of Rhenish pottery, the New Forest wares might be taken for the British version of vessels from the Marne or the Argonne. Their forms are shapely and sure, their decoration comparatively lifeless: Heywood Sumner, their excavator, observed that these works did not exhibit 'late-Celtic mastery of abstract line ornament, but fine perceptions of scale, spacing, emphasis, and restraint'. Though more varied, they did not range so far afield as the Castor ware. They were distributed throughout southern Britain, but they have no place in the Midlands and the North, and never reached the military market. Both the kilns and their output were less numerous; and the kilns, in small and isolated groups, were worked from huts so primitive as to suggest bothies and seasonal activity on a forest estate or public land. The impression created by this shifting, seasonal activity in the woodland is a little like that of charcoal-burning, and quite different from the old-established kiln-yards of the Castor potters' fields.

Apart from decorative wares, there was a vast output of kitchen wares and coarse table crockery indigenous to the province. As soon as the Roman armies arrived a profitable market was opened to such products, and the native potters were not slow to take advantage of the opportunity. At first they were content to supply vessels of their own type, though at once they improved the hardness of the pottery by using new technical processes. For some two generations wares of essentially Roman style and use, such as bowls for the table and kitchen mixing bowls, or mortaria, continued to be imported in bulk. Then they began to be copied. In four generations, by the middle of the second century A.D., the manufacture of common wares was entirely in provincial hands. The mixing bowls are stamped, in conformity with Roman practice, and, to judge from the stamps, most of the makers were natives, one or two of them endowed with Roman citizenship. The stamps attest a large number of makers; over sixty are known at Corbridge: but there was a big market to be supplied, over a long period, and many of the manufactories were small. How the commerce was conducted remains as yet obscure, but something is known of its ramifications. The northern military market, for example, was supplied by many northern potters, but Lincoln, Midlands, and even Middlesex potters took their share. Cooking-pots and jars, on the other hand, for which there was a much larger demand, were produced not only in small establishments but in very large ones, many of which are known by the wide distribution of their wares as opposed to the actual kilns. The extensive kiln-plants of Farnham (Surrey) supplied, with other unidentified establishments, the Thames valley market: but the Farnham wares have by no means the widest distribution of the comparable wares. The implication is that some vast potteries yet remain to be discovered. Sometimes, however, the military made their own vessels. The legionary kilns at the Holt, on the Dee, helped to supply the needs of the Twentieth Legion at Chester; the Ninth Legion, or part of it, was making pottery as well as tiles at Scalesceugh, near Carlisle; yet another legion seems to have manufactured attractive mica-dusted vessels for itself in the vicinity of Gloucester. Even at Ravenglass (Cumberland) an auxiliary regiment made some of its own pottery. Yet these instances, interesting though they be, are in fact the exceptions which prove the rule, that the military market normally drew its supplies of pottery from the civilian trader. The picture evoked is as complex as that of Samian ware. There is seen an abundance of small men, concerned with a local market and sometimes venturing to bid for a military order. But there are also the great contractors, some tied to the military market, others serving chiefly the great centres of civilian population, yet able to take a large military contract in their stride. The variation can be expressed in examples. The potteries of Knapton and

Crambeck both lie in east Yorkshire. Knapton cooking-pots are common in their home area, but do not stray far outside it. Crambeck wares are also well distributed in east Yorkshire, but they abound throughout the northern military area as well. An intermediate position is occupied by Derbyshire ware, which fills the unsophisticated farming settlements of the Pennine dales and reaches also Roman forts, but in much smaller quantity.

Legionary tileries have been incidentally mentioned, but there were many civilian establishments as well. An Imperial tilery existed near Calleva (Silchester) under Nero. The *colonia* of Glevum (Gloucester) made its own tiles, stamped *R(es) P(ublica) G(levensium)* and some-times bearing abbreviated names of its *duoviri quinquennales* (see p. 90). In the same district there was a private company, stamping with variant initials, much employed at Corinium (Cirencester). More interesting still are the stamped tiles from the villa of Ashtead (Surrey), which have been traced all over south-eastern Britain as far as Lincolnshire, Staffordshire, and Charterhouse on Mendip: many of the patterns are plain chevrons but there is a spirited initialled scene of wolf-hound and stag at bay, and some florid patterns with stiff but crowded conventional ornament, partly based upon standards of auxiliary regiments. This establishment was working from about A.D. 80 until after the middle of the second century A.D., and it is thought that it sent out journeymen to various parts of the province. Another but much more localized villa industry is that of Plaxtol (Kent), where the pattern was formed by the statement '*parietalem Cabriabanus fabricavit*' (Cabriabanus made this wall-tile), repeated.

Reference has already been made to the dearth of good stone for building and carving which obtains in south-eastern Britain, and which led subsequent ages to rob

Roman monuments so thoroughly of their stonework, ruining them in the process. In these circumstances the good stone of the Jurassic belt became an important article of commerce. Bath stone in particular was early discovered and exploited. Colchester tombstones destroyed in the Boudiccan revolt of A.D. 61 were made of this choice freestone, a point which shows how quickly the Roman *negotiator* or concessionnaire turned to profit the natural resources of the province. But the export of Bath stone was not confined to the earlier period. It was being used in Weston-under-Penyard (Herefordshire), in the third-century gates of Silchester, at Lydney, and in London. Ketton stone was used at Verulamium, Barnack rag in London.

In Yorkshire the stone slates of the West Riding went right across the county, to Wensleydale and to the Wolds. Extensive use was made in the Plain of York of the local deposits of gypsum, used for manufacturing the liquid plaster poured into coffins to preserve the dead; the result being the remarkable impressions of corpses in their shrouds which are preserved in the Philosophical Society's Museum at York.

Quern-stones for grinding grain have been little studied. By the army they were at first imported from the Andernach lava deposits of the Rhineland. But this was not continued. Hard British stones, such as millstone grit and pudding-stone, were being exploited later, and an interesting field of study here invites an attention it has not yet received. Whetstones form a smaller yet important group. Large numbers were on sale in the *forum* at Viroconium (Wroxeter) when it was burnt down in the later second century A.D. and these are thought to have come from Northamptonshire.

Salt had already been extensively worked on the Essex

coasts in the pre-Roman Iron Age, to which belong many of the so-called Red Hills, with their masses of broken burnt clay linings from evaporating furnaces used in boiling brine. The same process is attested for Roman times by its association with Roman pottery at Goldhanger (Kent), Canewdon (Essex), Cooling (Kent), and Dymchurch (Sussex). But geographical sources also mention at least two places called Salinae, where salt springs and brine pits must be in question. The first of these is Droitwich, of which the brine baths are still famous. The Romans presumably used them for salt production, since they do not attach to the name Aquae, signifiying a watering-place or spa. The second is at Middlewich in Cheshire, where lies the Roman site of Kinderton. A third Salinae is placed by the geographer Ptolemy in the canton of the Catuvellauni, and remains unidentified: the Catuvellauni do not appear to have extended to the east coast, and no important salt spring is now known in their area. Finally, in the *Digest*, as Mr Eric Birley has noted, there may be a reference to *salinae*, or salt-works, worked by convict labour, in the military area of northern Britain; and he observes that the context suggests the Firth of Forth, where the name Prestonpans commemorates later activity of the same kind. These various places cannot have been the only sites at which so indispensable a commodity was produced, but there is no suggestion that the output went elsewhere than to markets within the province.

One aspect of British economic life which deserves attention is the use of water-power machinery. This was not a marked feature of Mediterranean civilization, since the chief necessity, a constant supply of water, was so often lacking. But it was from the Mediterranean world that the under-shot water-wheel described by Vitruvius

was derived, and was used, for example, in aqueduct
overflows for grinding flour and cinnabar at Rome, or
for driving flour-mills near Arles in southern France. In
north-western Europe steady streams were more common, and Ausonius describes the saw-mills for marble on
the tributary River Ruwer in the Moselle valley. In
Britain examples are few but significant. The army was
driving flour-mills by water at three points on Hadrian's
Wall, using for the purpose respectively the North Tyne
and Irthing rivers and the Haltwhistle Burn. The stone
core of the water-wheel's hub still exists at the North
Tyne, and another hub-core of the same kind has recently
been found at Lincoln. At the villa of Woolaston Pill
power-driven stones were found re-used as flooring in a
building close to an artificial water-leet, while an iron
spindle for similar stones from Great Chesterford (Essex)
has been recognized in the Cambridge University
Museum of Ethnology and Archaeology. The wide distribution of these relics is impressive.

The imports of Roman Britain remained no more static
than the exports or the home-market. One of the oldest
and the most constant was wine, which was being imported long before the occupation on a fairly large scale
by a limited number of tribal chiefs. Not only did they
themselves esteem it, as the great storage-jars which fill
their tombs declare, but the custom of lavish hospitality
which it was a matter of prestige to indulge, demanded
substantial stocks. At least it was drunk both lavishly and
undiluted, with brutish consequences. When the conquest
came the amount of wine imported must have risen
sharply, since not only had a regular market been created
in advance, but this market must have been on the
increase. In addition, the troops, officials, and merchants
who crowded into the new province brought with them

a habitual taste for wine, which traders were ready to gratify. A coarse variety (*posca*) was an established part of the army ration. The only liquor which might rival it for consumption within the province was beer (*cervesa*), which in Britain, as in Gaul, was an esteemed drink, and unquestionably much cheaper. In Gaul, dark ale is mentioned as brewed in Trier (Augusta Treviorum); nothing is known of varieties of brew in Britain, but a fourth-century panegyrist mentions the two-fold use of grain, for bread and for beer. Wine, however, must have been the drink on all occasions with pretensions to elegance or culture, and this preference must have been of great value to traders. How much first-class wine reached Britain remains uncertain.

The imported wine no doubt continued to be carried in amphorae. But it should be recalled that in the Moselle valley, where wine was plentifully produced and exported in the second and third centuries A.D., barrels were also used, and barrels of Pyrenees fir from Silchester and London no doubt contained wine from Gascony which the Italian consumer rated as second-class. It seems certain that Aurelius Lunaris, ex-slave merchant of Lincoln and York, who erected an altar in Bordeaux following a safe sea-passage from York in A.D. 237, was representative of traders engaged in this traffic and shipping direct to the northern market, both military and civilian. Lunaris was a Briton: but the same view might well be taken of the presence of a Biturigan, Verecundius Diogenes from the Bourges district, among the same class of merchants of York, since wine forms by far the most likely article of trade between the two regions, both then and now. It should be added that vines would seem to have been grown in southern Britain, vine-stocks being reported from a villa at Boxmoor, in Hertfordshire. Britain is also

specifically mentioned as one of the provinces from which
restriction upon vine-growing was lifted in the third century A.D. But there is no archaeological evidence for production: neither vats nor presses have been identified,
and it seems clear that the climatic drawbacks must have
worked against successful or constant ventures of the kind.
Even if grown successfully, British grapes could seldom
have been produced in the quantity or quality required
for wine. It may be thought that such grapes as were produced were consumed as fruit, fresh or dried.

There was also a substantial import trade in olive oil,
much used for cooking but perhaps even more for light-
ing; and the stamps upon the great jars, or amphorae,
which contained it, come principally from the province of
Baetica in southern Spain. This importation flourished
chiefly in the first and second centuries A.D., and came to
an abrupt stop following the wholesale Imperial confiscation of these estates because their owners had supported
the British governor Albinus in his all but successful con-
test with Severus for the Empire. What took its place is
not apparent, but the very large volume of the trade must
have left a gap which required filling. Perhaps the olive
yards of southern France or Morocco filled the gap.
Certainly, whatever happened, the containers were now
different and there is a very marked drop in the number
of amphorae current. It may well be that candles, made
in the province, may have taken a more prominent place
as illuminants, while cooking fats, in which Britain must
have been very rich, may have taken the place of oil for
kitchen use.

If wine and oil were the principal imports for the table,
its furnishings at first came almost entirely from overseas.
The most costly and the most prized of table services were
undoubtedly the silver jugs, dishes, and cups or goblets.

These last were already being imported, if as rarities, in pre-Roman times. In the province, the silver plate which was the pride of every wealthy house in the Roman world came principally from the Mediterranean, though Gallic silversmiths were becoming important trade rivals. Some silver-ware must surely have been made in Britain, at such a centre as London. But surviving pieces follow classical models so closely that it is rarely possible to recognize a provincial copy. Silver-work which is certainly local, such as the silver decorative plaques from shrines or ritual furniture at Barkway and Stony Stratford, similarly follows the classical repertoire so faithfully as to lose much of the provincial character that it might have had. Only the provincial subject, as in the Capheaton *paterae*, enables a British piece to win recognition. Normally, then, it is difficult to identify British silver; and, while an east-Mediterranean origin must certainly be supposed for such a piece as the famous Corbridge *lanx*, a decorative tray which contains repeated references, both obvious and recondite, to Delos and its cults, it must be conceded that other vessels, especially those of the plainer sort, may have originated within the province. When potential craftsmanship is assessed the skill exhibited in beating, turning, and chasing the pewter table-services, which are patently British in origin, must be recognized and taken into account.

Bronze furnishings were also an important item in any list of imports. Among these figured elaborate table-lamps, candelabra, heated dishes, and containers, sets of strainers for wine, and finger-bowls. In the first century A.D. the bulk of these objects were indubitably imported, but gradually many of them came to be manufactured within the province; and there was an interesting half-way stage, during which Italian products were driven out of the market by Gallic merchandize. This is particularly noticeable in the bronze *pateiae*, used by civilians for heating wine and food, and by the army as mess-tins, which came almost exclusively from Campanian firms in the first century A.D., but carry more and more names of Gallic origin in the second. But details of British manufacture of metal bowls and dishes are also furnished by the remarkable series of stone moulds of white lias from Lansdown, near Bath. These exemplify not only the bowls themselves but details of the handles, medallions, and other ornamental features. The moulds seem to have been intended for beating rather than castings and it is not clear that the metallurgical work was done on the spot.

In addition to bronze table furnishings, decorated bronze work, both patterned and enamelled, poured in from Gallia Belgica. The foremost place was taken by the enamelled wine-ladles, cups, and jars; then came the rich enamelled brooches and belt-plaques; and next the gay bronze horse-trappings, for harness and saddle. Britain had indeed its own enamelled jewellery, particularly brooches; but these, lovely though they are, can hardly vie with the best work from Belgica, which belongs to the second and third centuries A.D. It is probably this, rather than British work, that is meant by Heliodorus, who assigns it to 'the barbarians who live on the borders of the Ocean', a phrase as applicable to Belgium as to Britain.

The Gallic capture of the Italian export trade in metal vessels is evident sooner and to far greater extent in the cheap ornamental table crockery known as Samian ware or terra sigillata, the brilliant red glazed pottery made both in plain vessels and in bowls covered externally with moulded decorative scenes or conventional patterns. The Italian centre of manufacture, at the height of its activity at the opening of the Christian era, lay at Arretium, the modern Arezzo, in Tuscany. Its products, decorated or otherwise, were closely modelled upon the metal vessels, of which they were intended to form a cheap copy in baser material, and the owners were Italian merchants working through slaves and freedmen. By the seventies of the first century A.D. wares of similar fabric were being so freely manufactured in Southern Gaul that they were actually flooding the Italian market. Their decoration is still classical in mode, though the figure themes become coarser in finish and decidedly less ambitious in scope, while conventional patterns acquire more flow and rest-lessness. From Southern Gaul production passed at the close of the first century A.D. to Central Gaul, and here the decorative motifs, while normally still derived from the classical repertoire, are used with still further freedom and a new abandonment of restraint. It can fairly be said that from now onwards, as the manufactories spread from Central Gaul to East Gaul and the Moselle valley (though Britain traded principally with Central Gaul), the patterns are employed with increasing incongruity and looseness, until the jumbled scenes become little more than texture, sometimes endowed with the accidental charm of a patchwork. The plain forms, too, gradually lose their sharp metallic outlines and assume shapes more adapted to the wooden forms upon which their moulds were made. Factories of Samian ware hardly spread to Britain. An East Gaulish manufacturer did, indeed, set up an establishment at Colchester, while individual moulds at York, Pulborough (Sussex), and certain ves-sels from Aldgate (London) suggest tentative attempts to introduce the process. More interesting perhaps are the native imitations of Samian decorated bowls which copy their form and reduce their pattern to a few simple strokes. These were current in the Midlands during the late first and early second century A.D. But British Samian ware was a drop in the ocean compared with the vast quantities of imported samian. The material is so common as to be the bane of museum curators, but to the archaeologist it is valuable indeed, since its ubiquity, its rapidly changing styles, its variety of makers' stamps, and its distinctive fabrics supply an unrivalled mass of datable material, often to be dated very closely indeed. The vast scale of importation may be gauged from the fact that no inhabited site in the province, whether farm, fort, village, or town, fails to yield Samian ware, often in great quantity. The army was certainly importing it in bulk, but how this traffic was organized and handled remains uncertain. For the civilian market it came in ship-loads, one of which, wrecked in the late second century A.D. near Whitstable (Kent), provided in later ages a name for Pudding Pan Rock.

Production of Samian ware was brought to an end by the invasion of Gaul in the later third century A.D. There was a revival of imitative fabrics in the Marne and Argonne regions in the fourth century A.D., with small conventional stamped patterns. In civilian areas of Britain this was widely imitated, particularly by the New Forest potteries. But it achieved a very considerable circulation in the south and comes as far north as York. In general, then, the gap was filled by now with various British decorated wares, but also by an increasing volume of imports of Rhenish glass ware and Rhenish glazed pottery decorated with white slip. The glass jugs and decanters, bowls, and plates, are among the most attractive of Roman provincial manufactures; and while their elegant undecorated forms are pleasant indeed, there are remarkable decorative effects in cutting and twisting and astonishing figured works, of which the Bacchic dance from Durnonovaria (Dorchester, Dorset) is a fine example. The models upon which these were based came from the east Mediterranean, and it may well be that the manufacturers themselves came from the same area. Their fidelity to classical models is unfailing. This glass importation did not, indeed, begin from the Rhineland. East Mediterranean plain bowls, dishes, and flasks of lovely translucent glass were already being imported in the first and second centuries A.D. The most ambitious were the cups embossed with circus scenes. But a special and attractive group was formed by multicoloured, or *mille-fiori*, pillar-moulded bowls and jars from Alexandria, imitating the fabulously expensive murrhine vessels made of reinforced fluorspar. They no doubt appealed especially to the polychromatic colour-sense of the Celtic world. Neither in the earlier nor even in the later period, however, was the volume of glass imported ever equal to that of Samian ware, but there was much more of it than is commonly supposed, as a survey of collections at York and Corbridge will reveal. It was also exported. Beyond the limits of the province, in northern Scotland, Roman glass of third and fourth centuries A.D. is not unknown, usually in connexion with burials, though it must always be recalled that this reflects in a rich grave the conditions of life in the circle of the deceased. The complete Turriff jug or the fragmentary painted cups, from Airlie and Kingoldrum in Angus and from Westray in Orkney, may be cited as examples; and the last-named introduce yet another variety of late-Roman glass, which selects for its painted subjects the beasts of the arena. These also were made in the Rhineland, and so far as is known no elaborate glass was manufactured in Britain.

The Rhenish pottery, on the other hand, is in form such

as might have been produced in Britain itself, and comprises jugs, beakers, and vases. The fabric is thin, with a highly polished dark colour coating, usually ornamented in simple running scrolls or medallions in white slip and also in barbotine. Sometimes the shoulder or belly of the vessel carries a terse, colloquial, and convivial inscription in white capital letters, such as 'suavis' (delicious!), 'da mi' (give it me!), 'misce mi' (mix it me!), 'vivatis' (long life to you!). The ware has a pleasant finish and attractive look. It is probably the kind mentioned in the famous inscription from the temple at Domburg in Walcheren, where a trader in pottery with Britain (*negotiator cretarius Britannicianus*) dedicated a statue of the local goddess Nehalennia 'because the goods had been preserved in good order' (*ob merces recte conservatas*).

Lamps of earthenware were also largely imported, much from Italy in the later first century A.D. and thereafter from southern Gaul where the industry flourished.

Certain more exotic imports should also be mentioned. Mediterranean marbles were imported for use at Londinium (London), Camulodunum (Colchester), Calleva (Silchester), Corinium (Cirencester), Lindum (Lincoln), and even at forts in the far north such as Banna (Bewcastle). They include porphyry from Egypt at Colchester, Silchester, and Canterbury; Carrara from Italy on monuments or public buildings at Colchester, Richborough, London, Silchester, Cirencester, St Albans, and Lincoln; Pyrenaean marble (*campon vert*) at Silchester; Peloponnesian marble (*verde antico*) at Bewcastle and also in the variety *rosso antico* at Lincoln; Euboean marble from Carystus (*cipollino*) at Cirencester. It would be wrong to overestimate the significance of such an item as marble, for the traffic can never have been large or even regular. But it is interesting to see how its use persisted and how the Mediterranean standards of culture adopted by the island demanded it. In the sixth century A.D. cultivated Britons still thought of themselves as *Romani* on the basis of language and literary tradition. But while the province existed there were many material links which might have justified the claim and this was one of them.

Another exotic import was papyrus from Egypt, which must have been in considerable demand, both by official bureaux, military and civil, for documents and by book-producers, whose skilled writers copied texts upon rolls.

Cinnabar (*minium*), which was an Imperial monopoly, was worked in Spain and treated in Rome. It was much used for painting the lettering of monumental inscriptions, and traces of it are not infrequently found. It represents another import which was rare but not negligible.

There was a limited but steady trade in cones of the stone pine for altar fuel and trade in incense must have been considerably larger. Cooking spices, notably pepper, ginger, and cinnamon, should be included: also perfumes in their glass phials, some from Imperial properties, such as the Judaean balsam groves, in their specially taxed containers, used both for the living and the dead.

No economic study of the province can be regarded as complete without reference to its coinage. A detailed study is here impossible, but there are some salient features which deserve emphasis. Britain seldom possessed an official mint. Only under the usurper-Emperors, Carausius (A.D. 287–93), Allectus (A.D. 293–6), and Magnus Maximus (A.D. 383–8), and during the years A.D. 296–324, under Constantius and Constantine I, was there such a mint on this side of the Channel. For supplies of coinage the province depended at first upon the Senatorial mint in Rome and the Imperial mint at Lugdunum (Lyons) and in the fourth century A.D. upon the mints of

Treviri (Trèves), Lugdunum (Lyons), and Arelate (Arles). At the period of conquest a flourishing native coinage, normally of gold and silver, but in Essex also of bronze, was in existence and had been actively circulating for at least fifty years over an area extending from Kent to the Cotswolds and the Wash and overlapping into Yorkshire. A substantial number of Roman Republican *denarii* had also been imported and accepted as part of the regular currency. Once the province was created, however, it would seem that tribes or client-kings were not allowed to continue coining, even Queen Cartimandua, beyond the garrisoned area, appears to have ceased her very limited issue. The result was that in the native areas the ancient coinage had to serve as the medium of exchange, with an admixture of newly introduced Roman bronze pieces, silver being the principal money of account. This use of pre-Conquest issues died out in most areas at the close of the first century A.D., when a debasement of the silver coinage by Trajan was preceded by calling in as much of the pre-existent coinage as possible. But in the backwoods of south Hampshire and Dorset, native coins continued to circulate until about the middle of the second century A.D. From the first, Roman bronze coinage was widely welcomed; and there was a great demand for the bronze issues of Claudius, owing to the exiguity of pre-existing supplies and the immense influx of troops. Copies were therefore extensively made; the best of them emanated from the legionary fortresses at Gloucester, Wroxeter, and Lincoln, and were in A.D. 71 transferred with the bank of the Ninth Legion to York; the less skilled versions were associated with tribal capitals. Once the province settled down and new supplies increased the issues in circulation, the copying virtually ceased and the volume of Roman silver and bronze steadily grew until the middle of the second century A.D. Only gold remained rare and hoards of it are confined to the military area. A possible exception in the matter of copying is afforded by the *Britannia* issues of Antoninus Pius, of which some are so poor in quality that they may well be products of a provincial mint.

From the middle of the second century A.D. onwards, there is a marked decline in the volume of currency, whatever the cause, a drop which reaches its nadir about A.D. 235. Now also the conservative attitude of the provincials towards the coinage becomes apparent, in a preference for the old-fashioned purer *denarius* as against the new double *denarius* or *antoninianus* of reduced weight and impure metal of Caracalla and his successors. This is evinced not only by the composition of hoards of savings, but by the large number of moulds for illicit casting of *denarii* belonging to the period. Much worse was to come. The ruinous invasions of the later third century A.D. meant that already under Gallienus (A.D. 259–68) the central authorities no longer made any attempt to retain the silver content of the *antoninianus*; and the Gallic Empire, to which Britain adhered, won initial prestige by keeping to better standards. When the Gallic coinage in turn collapsed, Britain was flooded with base issues, hoarded perhaps in the hope of their redemption for something better. The new reformed issue of Aurelian (A.D. 270–5), Probus, and Carus did not reach the province in sufficient quantity to drive out the base coinage, and even when the usurper Carausius (A.D. 287–93) began his rule by issuing fine silver *denarii*, the Gallic coinage types remained so familiar that they were copied in the bronze *minimi*, issued locally as small change during the eighties and nineties. But the return to the silver *denarius* demonstrates yet again the monetary conservatism of the province, and only when Carausius received recognition from the central government did his two mints adopt the Continental *antoninianus* of Diocletian and his colleagues, a policy continued by his supplanter Allectus (293–6).

The recovery of Britain by Constantius Caesar in A.D. 296 coincided with a new reform of the coinage, closely related to contemporary price-controls, in which large bronze or silver-washed bronze coins (*folles*) were issued at high face value but in highly artificial relation to a gold standard. These new coins were welcomed, as representing a sound currency, and local issues of large copies were made in an attempt to resist reduction in their size. It is noteworthy that later, whenever a return was made to this size, even under the Gallic usurper Magnentius (A.D. 350–3), such coins were well received in Britain. At the same time the need for smaller denominations was still met by the continued circulation of the radiate Gallic issues, and by the issues of *minimi*, the minute copies of them. Constantius had one stationary mint in Britain, at London, and more than one travelling establishment. Constantine retained the London mint until A.D. 324, but his monetary policy was markedly different, since he brought the bronze coinage back to its metal value and drove out the over-tariffed heavy issues in an attempt to counteract the catastrophic rise in prices, which had been aided by the gap between the face value and real value of the coinage. The monetary history of the next forty years is in fact that of a fight between the two tendencies, the first to over-tariff the coinage and endeavour to fix prices, the second to bring the coinage back to real value and let prices find their level. The period was one of internal calm, only broken by the effects of the revolt of Magnentius (A.D. 350–3), which Britain joined, not without throwing up two minor usurpers, Carausius II and Genseris, who seem to have favoured the central government or hoped for recognition from it.

About A.D. 348, a tendency to restrict the volume of currency in circulation had become apparent, and subsisted until after the disasters of A.D. 367–9, when the new and profuse bronze coinage of Valentinian I, emitted by the mints of Arles and Lyons, began to spread widely over the province. A new phenomenon, too, is the silver coinage of Treviri (Trèves), which now became the principal silver-issuing mint of Gaul. No doubt this mint was supplied by silver from Gaul itself, but it is likely that the British lead-silver mines, worked by the *curiales*, also made an important contribution, which seems to have been paid for by the State in silver coinage. Britain at this period exhibits a wealth of silver and even gold coinage unexampled in any other western province. But the closing of all the Gallic mints in A.D. 395 meant an end both of this enterprise and of regular supplies of coinage, and in the matter of currency the province had now to subsist upon what it could make or adapt by clipping or restriking from older issues. It is the dearth of precisely-dated coinage after A.D. 395, except in the rare gold and silver issues, which makes the evidence for the numismatic history of the final phases of Roman and sub-Roman Britain, as reflected in the bronze coinage, so difficult to interpret. Current opinion is divided between views which favour, on the one hand, a continuation of debased and reduced issues of coinage until the sixth century A.D., and, on the other, a cessation of such issues soon after the middle of the fifth century A.D. The content of this late coinage is not in doubt. It comprises copies of third-century radiate types, of the coins of Constans and

of those of the House of Theodosius. There are widely
differing degrees of skill and style in the copies; and perhaps the most striking and dramatic feature is the reduction of size in some cases to 'minimissimi', coins so minute
that fifty-one of them will cover a halfpenny. It is also
certain that all the striking degradations of style and
module have already appeared before the close of the
fourth century A.D. The determining factors for dating
thus become such questions as relative wear and devolution of types, but, above all, the archaeological associa-
tions of the coins; and more material and study will be
required before these can be decisively interpreted. On
the other hand, the bulk of authentic Theodosian issues
is so large in the area of the Home Counties as to suggest
that active commercial enterprise, including close connexion with the Continent through Rutupiae (Richborough), was continuing until the third decade of the
fifth century A.D. This continuation has been used to
support the view of a re-occupation of the province; but
it is in fact economic evidence, and does not illuminate
the political scene. The continuing economic activity is
further supported by the silver hoards of the worn and
clipped *siliquae* which served as money of account in the
absence of further new supplies. These fan out from the
Home Counties to Somerset, Lancashire, and north
Yorkshire and must indicate provincial communities still
economically active until A.D. 420–30, whatever their
political state may have been.

CHAPTER FIVE

RELIGIOUS CULTS

THE religions of Roman Britain divide into four categories; the official religion practised by Roman and provincial civilians, the cults native to the province, and the cults of the Roman army, official and otherwise.

One side of the official religion has earned considerable notoriety because it is enumerated by Tacitus among the causes of the Boudiccan revolt in A.D. 61: this is Emperor-worship. It is clear that the Roman government introduced in Britain, as in other western provinces, the worship of the Emperor to serve as a unifying focus of loyalty and of gratitude for the *pax Romana*. In Gaul an annual religious gathering replaced an annual tribal convention of Druidical origin, and the institution worked well; partly because it was continuing a tradition, if in new form, and partly because there was a large number of participant tribes, sixty-four in all, over which the cost could be spread. In Germany it worked less well; for it was not traditional, while the tribes concerned were much fewer in number. In Britain, most tribes had certainly paid dues to Druids, as the finds from Llyn Cerrig tell us, but their political rivalries must have made impossible any united council, and by A.D. 61 there cannot have been much more than ten tribes participating in the worship. These cults were costly. There was the central temple at Camulodunum (Colchester) to build and maintain, and excavations show that it was a large and sumptuous building upon which no expense was spared. It occupied a large court and in front of it there stood a great altar, flanked by statue-bases, a design reminiscent of the Gallic altar of Rome and Augustus, as shown on coins. The British cult, however, was a personal cult of the Emperor Claudius, to whom it accorded divinity during his lifetime with an emphasis which went well beyond previous Roman practice. Claudius and his plenipotentiaries had been permitted to organize the province without referring back to the Senate and this may be recognized as one of the consequences. The observances of any established Imperial cult were numerous and ran in calendared order throughout the year. The tribal aristocrats who undertook by election the priesthoods of the cult for a year were accordingly expected not only to reside at Camulodunum throughout their term of office but to pay for festivals and games associated with the honour but not part of provincial expenditure. 'In the guise of religion the chosen priests poured out their whole fortunes' is the Tacitean picture of their plight; and it is not surprising that some Britons at least found the new religion too heavy a strain upon purse and personality. It represented altogether too sharp and burdensome a transition into Roman state religion. After the rebellion, in which the temple perished in flames, the cult was certainly established afresh. It has, however, been regarded as doubtful whether it continued long at Colchester, in view of the concentration of the government of both procurator and provincial legate in London. All analogy would indeed suggest that the provincial worship will have been associated with the provincial capital. Proof is indeed wanting, but it may be regarded as likely that about the end of the first century A.D. the provincial cult moved to the administrative centre.

In the Roman *coloniae* or chartered towns, a temple in honour of living and deceased members of the Imperial

House was an essential. The worship was undertaken by a statutory group of six priests, drawn from wealthy freedmen traders, this being one of the duties which the community felt that new and rich citizens should bear. These men might also be expected to give games or to pay for festivals, but they were certainly called upon to undertake less obvious but useful and expensive public benefactions, such as street repairs, bridges, or sewers. This Roman conception of the duty of a rich citizen makes it easier to understand the line taken with tribal notables, and in Roman society the idea was understood and taken for granted. Accordingly, the *Seviri Augustales*, six priests for the Imperial cult, appear both at Lincoln and at York; indeed, one wealthy trader, in A.D. 237, was a *sevir Augustalis* of both cities. It is no doubt entirely due to chance that evidence for similar bodies has not yet appeared from Colchester to Gloucester.

The Imperial cult was an observance intended directly to promote the safety and welfare of the Roman state, and it was therefore a matter of immediate concern to communities of Roman citizens to see it regularly observed. From the provincials, of whom until A.D. 213 few were Roman citizens, what was required was an expression of loyalty. This was achieved, not merely by the annual public vows for the Emperor's safety, but by linking the worship of the Emperor's *numen*, or spiritual power, with public and private dedications. The process is well illustrated by the dedication of the temple of Neptune and Minerva at Noviomagus (Chichester), which the smiths' guild made 'for the welfare of the Divine House by the authority of Tiberius Claudius Cogidubnus, King and Imperial legate in Britain'. Here the famous client-king, whose loyalty was irreproachable, is securing that the foundation of a temple by a gild should voice their loyalty to the Emperor. A statue-base dedicated to Nero is also known from Chichester, and later still a second public religious monument was dedicated 'in honour of the Divine House'. The procedure may be compared with the dedication of a new theatre-stage in A.D. 138–61 by a magistrate of the *vicus Petuarensis*, the village-metropolis of the Parisi (p. 80), 'In honour of the Divine House of the Emperor Antoninus Pius and to the Imperial spirits'. The *numen Augusti* or *numina Augustorum* could thus be worshipped either by themselves or in association with other gods and nothing is more frequent throughout the province than this association of the Emperor's spirit and gods of every kind. An act of divine worship is thus coupled with an act of devotion to the Emperor, whose spiritual power and majesty is thereby enhanced. The frequency of the custom is a tribute to the readiness with which the province as a whole came presently to a loyal acceptance of Emperor-worship, despite an ill-omened start.

In addition to the worship of the Emperor, there was the worship of the State deities of Rome, in particular the Capitoline triad, Jupiter, Juno, and Minerva, not to mention Mars and Victory, Neptune, Apollo, Vulcan, Ceres, Mercury, and others. These were regularly worshipped in the *coloniae* of Roman citizens and in the capital, and this meant the creation of colonial and provincial *flamines*, or high-priests, who would be Roman citizens. At *Lindum colonia* there is a trace of corporate worship of both Apollo and Mercury by the different *vici* or wards of the town. Here also appear the Parcae, or Fates, worshipped by an official of a burial-club. A fine relief of Abundantia or a comparable personification introduces yet another typically Roman conception. There is also an elegant relief of a tutelary deity belonging to a quadrangular monument which might well be part of a Column to Jupiter, of the type described below. At Camulodunum a statue of Victory is mentioned by Tacitus, and a fine head of Claudius is known. At Eburacum (York) literature similarly records a shrine of Bellona, the Goddess of War, and there is a noble head of Constantine Caesar.

As the provincials themselves became Roman citizens, all free-born becoming such in A.D. 213, the worship of Roman deities must have become still more widely diffused. There are signs of this in important provincial towns. Corinium (Cirencester) has yielded the base of a column to Iuppiter Optimus Maximus, restored by a fourth-century governor. Noviomagus (Chichester) has produced a similar and earlier dedication. This form of the cult is an interesting one, since it brings Britain into a North-West European circle of belief, in a rider god who trod down the powers of the underworld under his feet and who early became identified with the Roman Iuppiter. Much earlier Minerva and Neptune had been adopted in the capital of Cogidumnus, as patron deities of the manufacture and sea-borne traffic of a gild of iron-workers.

But in the cantonal capitals an unadulterated acceptance of purely Roman cults is rare. The canton itself might be represented, as at Silchester, by a *Genius* or *Tutela* with mural crown. At Silchester also, there are traces of a cult of Mars, not necessarily a war-god in a Celtic environment. Hercules too appears, but only as equated with Segomo, undoubtedly a Celtic god. At Corinium Dobunnorum (Cirencester) the famous group of Matres, probably the Suleviae, represents a cult of the Gallic mother-goddess, usually depicted in triplicate to indicate her power. The three goddesses sit stiff and prim, as British as they can be. There was also a cult of mother-goddesses with children playing at their feet, comparable with the Nursing Mother-goddesses (*nutrices*) of Pannonia and evidently another native manifestation of the mother-cult, in Roman representational form. At Verulamium the so-called triangular temple has been tentatively identified with a cult of Cybele, but the identification is admittedly far from secure. More interesting is the Mithraic token, as one of the rare relics of the cult of Mithras in such an environment. At Wroxeter a temple of Mediterranean form yielded fragments of life-sized statues of a god or gods connected with horses, and a remarkable piece of small-scale sculpture, depicting an emblem of fertility driving a four-horse chariot, and no doubt representing an aspect of the god there worshipped. In Isurium Brigantum (Aldborough) the tutelary deity of the canton, Brigantia, must have been worshipped, though the town has yet yielded no record of the cult. Her statue, reproduced at Birrens, is a remarkable personification, which combines in one figure the conception of a territorial goddess, with mural crown, a war-goddess clad like Minerva but with an auxiliary regiment's type of helmet, a Victory with wings, and a featureless monolith representing Caelestis. Brigantia, whose cult is discussed further below (p. 198), is elsewhere addressed as a water-goddess; but there is no suggestion of a connexion with water in the Birrens figure, nor is there any hint of the masculinity with which this deity is once endowed in an inscription. Native belief must have lain behind the conception, in part, but many of the epithets and the entire translation of them into stone are wholly Roman in idiom. Another native cult associated with a northern native capital is represented by the ritual bucket and sceptres crowned with busts of Mars which

went into the grave of a second-century dignitary of
Petuaria (Brough on Humber). At Venta Silurum
(Caerwent) one of the local deities, connected with a
gild, was Mars Ocelus Vellaunus, equated with the
Moselle valley god Mars Lenus. Mars Lenus was closely
connected with healing rather than with war, and it may
be presumed that Mars the 'Lofty' or 'Holy', which is the
meaning of Ocelus, and 'Superior', which is the meaning
of Vellaunus, was a deity of the same kind, whose activities were not exclusively connected with war, however
useful they might be in it.

The deities of the native capitals merge imperceptibly
with those of the countryside, and so also do their buildings. The native type of temple, of which an early Iron-
Age example built in timber was discovered on the
site of London Airport, took in Britain and Gaul the
form of a high sanctuary surrounded by a portico
in which offerings or the god himself could be exhibited
and from which a large body of worshippers might be
addressed. The sanctuary was the dwelling of the god or
gods concerned and was not intended to hold a congrega-
tion. It was lighted from high windows above the surrounding portico, but these were sometimes small and
often open, serving essentially to light the shrine but not
to floodlight or to display its contents. In the Roman
province the form continued and had a long life, and the
same type of building was adapted to both round and
multangular plans. There is no need to think of these
modifications as due to Roman influence, and it may be
surmised that round prototypes at least will in time be
found: one has, indeed, been suspected at Maiden Castle.
Builders in the Roman manner were, however, able to
enlarge the scale of the building and to bring to its
embellishment many new materials. One of the pre-

VERANDAH

CELLA

Entrance

FOREBUILDING

10 ⌊⌊⌊⌊⌊⌊⌊⌊⌊⌊ 0 ⌊_____⌊ 10 ⌊_____⌊ 20 Feet

Figure 12. Harlow, the Romano-British version of a
Celtic temple

Roman customs had been to decorate such buildings with
freshly severed human heads; 'a sickening sight till one
got used to it', remarked a Greek traveller in Gaul.
Carving and painting inspired by Roman architectural
models would be an improvement upon this. Thus civilized, the type was widespread. At Silchester all the known

temples, three square and one multangular, follow the
native pattern, but their decoration was highly Romanized. At Verulamium one of the oldest and most important temples in the town was of the rectangular box-type,
though it was later extended by adding side wings which
replaced the portico. This was no doubt a more convenient way of conserving and exhibiting the offerings of
the faithful. The most northerly example, recently
detected by air-photography, lies west of the military
supply-depot at Corbridge (Northumberland). Reference has already been made to examples of such temples
in hill-fort sites, but there are many others. One of the
most remarkable, also noted above, is at Gosbecks Farm,
near Colchester, while two more shrines of the same kind
exist at Sheepen, still nearer the town. These, as often
happened with country shrines, were enclosed in their
own precinct wall; and it is the fact that they are placed
so as to avoid the dominating position within the enclosure which suggests their association with groves or
open-air statues or the like. Dedications from Colchester
shrines are known. Gosbecks was associated with Mercury, and a building nearer the town was also dedicated
to Silvanus, with the native title of Callirius. This name
is not known in Gaul, but of the native epithets Toutates
and Alator from Barkway the former is well known in
North-East Gaul, and his presence indicates that Camulos was not the only deity whom the Catuvellauni brought
across with them. But there were connexions also with the
outlands of the province, obscure though they be. Nodens
at Lydney has his counterpart in Irish legend, Nuada of
the Silver Hand; the sphere of Maponus, the native god
of youth and music whose worship centres in northern
Britain, probably lay as much outside the province as in
it; Mars Medocius Campesium was worshipped by a

Caledonian at Colchester, and may be reckoned as imported by him. Some deities were imported in Roman times. Such were Mars Rigisamus from Aquitania, worshipped at West Coker (Somerset); and Mars Leucetius, worshipped with Nemetona at Bath by a Gaul from the Moselle valley, both being Rhineland deities. The Matres also are thought to be imported, but if so they found a place very deep in provincial affection.

Often, however, it is a local god or godling to whom the shrine belongs. The highly complicated deity at Maiden Castle, a Trinity of Bull, Female, and Owl, has already been noted; Ancasta, the goddess of Bitterne; the nameless goddess who broods ominous and hag-like on the New Forest jar-cover from Linwood, published by Professor Hawkes; Sul Minerva, the splendid goddess who presided with a sort of Pre-Raphaelite dignity over the hot spring at Bath, or Arnemetia who performed the same function at Buxton. The ritual crowns or head-dresses associated with such shrines are also worth passing note. Lydney yielded at least three fine ones, with scenes from the cult-legends of Nodens upon them. The shrine of Jupiter and Vulcan at Stony Stratford (Buckinghamshire) yielded an elaborate head-dress of chains and plaques. A head-dress of the same kind was found at Cavenham Heath (Suffolk), with another crown largely stripped of its ornaments. It seems clear that many of the small silver appliqué ornaments decorated with gods and goddesses come from similar ritual vestments.

In northern Britain, where the military area has yielded the bulk of Romano-British inscriptions, there are a large number of shrines dedicated to local gods and godlings: and these must in some sense serve as a pattern for the many similar sanctuaries of which no record has survived in the south. At Condercum (Benwell), on

Hadrian's Wall, the temple survives, a small building with apse at one end and a side doorway. Two fine altars flanked the apse, dedicated by commandants of the fort, specifying the godling here worshipped as Antenociticus or Anociticus respectively. His life-sized stone statue stood in the apse, but only fragments of limbs survive and a remarkable head which portrays a youthful god of wild aspect, with hair so thick and tousled as to suggest a bear-skin, and a torque about his neck. At Brocolitia (Carraw-burgh) the sacred spring of Coventina, which still bubbles up limpid in its stone tank, was covered by a temple of Celtic type in which the well or open basin took the place of a central shrine. Into the basin had been thrown not only offerings of money and knick-knacks, but eventually many of the altars and sculptured tablets from the temple. This happened early in the fifth century A.D. and was done so deliberately as to raise the question whether Christians did it. The sculptures illustrate Coventina sometimes as a gracious nymph, sometimes a single figure, sometimes raised to the power of three, but always reclining on a water-borne leaf. The offerings, nearly all bronze coins or pins and brooches, indicate a humble body of worshippers and the picture is completed by two home-made incense-burners, plainly the work of a votary who fashioned them and had them baked in a local kiln or oven. Three other local gods had a wider distribution. Maponus, who was worshipped at Rib-chester, Castlesteads, and Corbridge, was equated with Apollo Citharoedus, or Apollo the bard, who sang to the harp. His holy place, the Locus Maponi, lay north of Hadrian's Wall and has been identified with the Cloch-mabonstane, a megalithic circle on the north shore of the Solway which was in post-Roman times still the tra-ditional site for Border meetings. It was doubtless in his aspect of patron of peaceful festivities that Maponus found a place in the Roman pantheon. Cocidius, on the other hand, whose shrine, the Fanum Cocidi, also lay north of the Wall, was a god equated with Mars, and the silver plaques from Bewcastle which depict him show him in full armour with a spear of native type. His worship clusters thick in the basin of the Cumberland Irthing and to north of it. When it spreads out eastwards the god loses his identity as Mars and becomes equated with Silvanus, as if he were there the god of the wild. Once, too, he is given the name of another local deity, Vernostonus, at Ebchester. The identity of this god as a war-god is not in doubt, and his name appears to mean, consonantly, 'the red one': it has nothing to do with the River Coquet. The third god is more exclusively Cumbrian, and his worshippers, to judge from their small and graceless altars, of humbler sort. This was Belatucadrus, who is also equated with Mars, but in the absence of a representation and in view of the lack of direct connexion with war which characterizes many of the Celtic deities thus equated, it will be wiser to suspend judgement as to his sphere of activity. Godlings there were in plenty. The local aspects of Silvanus, connected with hunting in the high Pennines, have already been noted (p. 144). Contrebis at Overborough (Lancashire); Mars Condatis at Piercebridge and Chester-le-Street (both Co. Durham), connected with a watersmeet at each; Verbeia, goddess of the Wharfe, at Olicana (Ilkley, Yorkshire); Setlocenia at Alauna (Maryport, Cumberland); Vanauns at Castlesteads (Cumberland). Some of these are river-gods, and on the Tyne Bridge at Pons Aelius (Newcastle upon Tyne), where the tides and the river met, Ocean and Neptune were worshipped in a bridge-chapel or sanctuary.

Finally, there is the cult of Brigantia, of which the

distribution divides sharply into two regions. There are the frontier dedications by troops or civilians, the former occurring at Birrens (Dumfriesshire) and at Corbridge, the latter in the Castlesteads area (Cumberland) and at South Shields (Co. Durham). These dedications are explicable as placating the *genius loci*, and a civilian dedication in the same sense comes from Adel (Yorkshire). But the second group of dedications, from the Calder basin, is erected by Roman citizen civilians, one at least dating before the general extension of citizenship in A.D. 213, who have the air of army veteran settlers. If so, the dedications would represent shrines connected with land settlement, honouring the patron goddess of that particular countryside.

In southern Britain, many sumptuous shrines now lack their dedications and there is left only the evidence of devotion and a heavy capital outlay. The elaborate octagonal temple at Weycock (Berkshire) or at Pagan's Hill (Somerset) and the sanctuaries at Jordan's Hill (Dorset) and Woodeaton (Oxfordshire) have not yet afforded any precise indication of the deity worshipped in them. The dearth of building stone in the most civilized part of the island and the consequent robbing of Roman stonework has affected knowledge of these matters regrettably. There are also the scattered objects, now divorced from shrines, which have something to tell of individuals and their beliefs. Such are the fine statuettes of Jupiter, from Earith (Huntingdonshire) and Ranksborough Hill (Rutland), or of the Emperor Nero, from Barking Hall (Norfolk). The three richly decorated silver *paterae* from Capheaton (Northumberland) depict scenes connected with the army and commerce and with Hercules who united them both. The gold and silver *patera* from Backworth (Northumberland) was given by a Roman citizen to the Matres. The Mithraic figure from Whitton, Ipswich, recalls the imported Eastern cult associated with army or mercantile circles. The London marble statue of a river-god indicates the cult of the Thames; the London flagon which mentions a temple of Isis, commemorates the worship particularly associated with commerce from overseas and with shipping firms. The mosaic pavement of the Gnostic believer at Brading (Isle of Wight), or the Bacchic and Orphic pavements from Somerset point again, as noted above, to individual tastes and to those cults, which, like Christianity, set a standard of individual behaviour and salvation which was hard to follow but stimulating to possess. Of Christianity little survives. The written references to British bishops at the Councils of Arles (A.D. 314), Nicaea (A.D. 325), Sardica (A.D. 343), and Ariminum (A.D. 349) are supplemented archaeologically by the church at Calleva (Silchester) and the remarkable Christian wall-paintings recently recovered from a rich man's villa at Lullingstone (Kent). The Christian mosaic from Frampton, or the hallowing by crosses of a fountain at Chedworth seem also to indicate Christian families of villa owners. Christian finger-rings are possessions so personal as to be considered certain indicators of the religion of their owners, just as Christian formulae upon Cumberland or Westmorland tombstones suggest the same thing. But much of the evidence, consisting of the use of Christian emblems upon manufactured objects, proves little more than the existence of an atmosphere or climate not unfavourable to the religion which the Emperor had adopted. It may have little or no bearing upon the actual beliefs of the buyer. What remains indelibly impressive is the importance which the Church attached to the suppression of the British heresy of Pelagianism, and the fact that a well-attended con-

ference on the subject could be held at Verulamium
almost a generation after the Imperial government had
ceased to function in the province.

The civilian world had its regulated and calendared
observances, but these are obscured both by lack of direct
evidence and by the large number of private, sporadic,
and occasional dedications. The military world also displays an abundance of dedications of the latter class, but
there was so large a number of regiments, each with its
official cults, that the chance of survival is greater and the
picture so much the more complete. In Britain the class
of soldiery about whose worship least is in evidence is
that of the Roman citizen troops, the legionaries, quartered for most of the period of existence of the province at
the three great fortresses, Caerleon, Chester, and York.
Between them, these fortresses afford a fleeting glimpse
of official religion. A dedication to the legionary standards at Chester and the fragmentary door-posts of a subsidiary shrine in the administrative offices of the headquarters at Caerleon are almost all that remain of the
wealth of official dedications which such buildings elsewhere have produced in more favourable conditions. A
rich altar dedicated by a *tribunus militum* to the *genius
loci* for the safety and welfare of two Emperors in the
early third century A.D., a clerk's dedication to Minerva
and a senior centurion's altar to Juppiter Tanarus are the
outstanding individual dedications from Chester, and the
York fortress yields no better results. Only at sites where
legionaries are out-stationed do reflections of the cults of
their base-fortresses appear. At Corbridge (Northumberland), for example, the elaborate furnishings of a third-
century headquarters commemorate, first, the standard
of the detachment, with a decorative reference to the public festival of the Rosaliae, when the standards were

garlanded with roses for worship, and, secondly, the worship of Hercules, which was inextricably connected with the cult of the Emperor and the duties and labours of his army. There appear also statues of the Capitoline deities, a remarkable decorative panel and pediment from a shrine of Dea Roma, and also statues of the *genius* or guardian deity who presided over the individual unit or its station. At Newstead (Roxburghshire) a centurion commanding a detachment in garrison dedicates in the headquarters an altar to Iuppiter Optimus Maximus, the god who had so successfully guided the destiny of Rome for centuries. An out-stationed soldier on special duties at Dorchester (Oxfordshire) dedicated an altar and the screens round it to Iuppiter Optimus Maximus, reverenced in the office or post of which he had charge. The eagle of Jupiter crowned the legionary standard and so often crowned it with Victory. The goddess of Victory thus came to be associated with each legion, and a silver arm, torn from a half-scale statue of the Victory of the Sixth Legion, demonstrates how costly and valuable the more portable offerings might be. Amid this array of official deities the Emperors had their due place, both on the decorative plaques of the standards and in the regimental shrine, where the statue of the reigning Emperor occupied a chief position.

The auxiliary regiments, recruited from non-Roman provincials, provide in Britain a wider field. Their regimental shrines did not house dedications to Jupiter, but contained altars to the guardian deity of the Emperor and of the regimental standards, or to the Emperor's Discipline, 'The Empire's strongest bond', as a Roman once called it. Most of them contained a life-sized bronze statue of the reigning Emperor, of which fragments have occasionally been found, as at Carvoran, or its great base,

as at Bewcastle (Cumberland). When Emperors multi-
plied, as in the fourth century A.D., their statues might
have to be placed at the approach to the sanctuary, as at
Risingham (Northumberland) or Brough by Bainbridge
(Yorkshire), or the shrine itself might be enlarged, as at
Corbridge (Northumberland). In addition there were the
standards to be housed, and in order that the chapels
might display effectively all that they contained, they
were often equipped with raised platforms (*suggestus*)
inside them and open fronts marked by low decorative
screens, beyond which the holy things might be seen.

But if Jupiter found no place in the regimental shrine,
he and the appropriate associated deities had their recognized place upon the parade-ground, where the commandant of the regiment, acting on its behalf and in its
presence, took the annual vows for the welfare and safety
of the State on the 1st January and for the Empire and
Emperor two days later. Here, year in year out, new
altars to Iuppiter Optimus Maximus, the guardian deity
of the Roman State, were erected and the old ones
solemnly and reverently buried below ground. Few of
these buried groups of altars have been discovered, for
they left above ground even in Roman times no indication of their presence. But a remarkable group from
Alauna (Maryport, Cumberland) and a chance find at
Camboglanna (Birdoswald) belong to this category, and
such groups may well be there to find at every fort, if
chance permitted their recovery. The Maryport set,
though manifestly incomplete, forms an excellent representative example and is worth description. The most
numerous class is formed by dedications to Iuppiter
Optimus Maximus, plainly representing the annual vows
and offered both by the commandant personally and by
the unit corporately. Normally Jupiter holds the field

alone, but he is occasionally and significantly coupled
with the *numen Augusti* both by commandant and regiment, as also at other forts; and one commandant dedicated a building or, more probably, a *tribunal,* or
parade-ground platform, to Iuppiter Capitolinus for the
welfare of Antoninus Pius (A.D. 137–61). The repetition
of dedications and dedicators, related to the annual
renewal of vows, is frequent; five officers in particular
recur three or four times upon different stones, and the
units dedicating corporately are repeated many times
also. In addition to the altars of Jupiter, there are altars
to Mars, with the highly significant qualification of *mili-
taris,* to distinguish him from non-military types of this
god, such as have been already mentioned (p. 190).
Victoria Augusta, Imperial Victory, is another complementary dedication of which a duplicate is extant. Plainly
the series is incomplete, but it gives a highly interesting
and important picture of the annual ceremonies. A vivid
literary record of the same thing is furnished by the so-
called Feriale Duranum, a calendar of official festivals
(*feriae*) of the Twentieth Cohort of Palmyrenes from Dura
on the Euphrates, dated to soon after A.D. 225. The altars
belong to a special occasion, but the calendar reveals how
every week brought its own religious celebrations which
it was the duty of the regiment to observe and which
linked its traditions with the public worship of the Roman
state. That other festivals not covered by the surviving
portions of the Feriale were observed is shown by the
Derventio (Papcastle, Cumberland) dedication dated to
19 October, the Armilustrium. The third-century altar
from Borcovicium (Housesteads, Hadrian's Wall), set up
'to gods and goddesses according to the interpretation of
the oracle of the Clarian Apollo', is a particularly interesting special case, in which an oracular instruction was

implemented by Imperial order officially throughout the whole Empire.

The parade-grounds themselves leave little visible trace, except on hilly sites, where they happen to be deliberately cut and levelled; a fine example of this kind appears at Hardknott (Cumberland) and another at Tomen-y-mur (Merionethshire), while one at Maryport (Cumberland) was destroyed in the nineteenth century. All are, or were, large levelled areas, about 100 yards square, suitable either for squad drill or a general parade. Traces of a *tribunal* in the centre of one side have been noted at Hardknott and Maryport. They had their own deities, the Campestres, mother-goddesses in origin and no doubt imported into official religion by the Celtic regiments which even filled the drill-book with many of their own terms of command. The Campestres are normally associated with cavalry. At Condercum (Benwell, Northumberland) they are worshipped together with the *genius alae*. There must also be reckoned the deities disturbed by the reconstruction of a deserted fort, as at Newstead, where Diana and Silvanus, patrons of the wild who had taken temporary possession of the site, were honoured by the commandant of the new garrison. Sometimes an officer arriving in the new land would dedicate personally a whole series of altars to deities of local significance, as did Cocceius Firmus at Auchendavy on the Antonine Wall. Or such personal dedications might be made on completion of a term of office.

Within the fortress or fort most buildings had their presiding deity or genius. The commandant in his own house worshipped the *genius praetori* among the household gods (*lares*), called in a Greek inscription at York 'the gods of the general's *praetorium*'. The military clerks, working in the unit's record-office, or the pay-clerks, in the regimental bank, erected altars to Minerva. Each of the *centuriae* into which an infantry regiment was divided, or each *turma* of a cavalry unit had its *genius*, presiding over the barrack-block, a deity sometimes rendered in classical convention and sometimes descending to a comfortable everyday level. In the stables, Epona, the goddess of ostlers, would find her place, as at Carvoran. The fort bath-house came within the purview of Fortuna, not because games of chance were often played there, but because naked man was particularly vulnerable to the powers of evil and required protection. Sometimes this Fortune is called Augusta, sometimes Conservatrix, always with the intention of emphasizing her power. Occasionally she is portrayed as a statue in person, graciously enthroned, with her particular emblems or attributes at her feet.

Outside the fort and beyond the range of the parade-ground an auxiliary unit might worship collectively the gods of its homeland, brought with it from overseas. At Vinovia (Binchester, Co. Durham) the ala Vettonum, from north-east Spain, was worshipping the *Matres Ollototae sive transmarinae*, a useful if slightly inaccurate interpretation of the Celtic word, which means 'of the foreign folk'. A famous case is the Tungrians at Blatobulgium (Birrens, Dumfriesshire) who brought with them their god Mercury and their goddesses Viradechthis and Harimella. The Dea Hammia, imported by the Syrian archers to Carvoran, is another case, matched by Virgo Caelestis or Dea Syria, to whom a famous metrical hymn was dedicated by the commandant of the fort. Mogons was introduced from the Middle Rhine by the Vangiones at Risingham (Northumberland), the Matres Alateivae from the Lower Rhine by Gauls at Cramond (Midlothian). Apollo Anextlomarus from Eastern Gaul appears at South Shields and the Gallic god of victory, with his storks, at Chesterholm and Risingham. Another important introduction of the same kind was effected in northern Britain during the third century A.D., by the irregular levies from the Germanic fringes of the Empire. The Frisii from beyond the lower Rhine brought to Borcovicium (Housesteads, Northumberland) Mars Thincsus and his attendant female godlings, the Alaisiagae, four of whose names, each more outlandish than the last, are preserved. A second irregular unit, the numerous Hnaudifridi, called after its native chief, also participated in the cult. But whatever may be thought of the names of deities and dedicators, the barbarisms cease when representations are required. Thincsus emerges as Mars in full armour and with attendant goose, while the Alaisiagae hover, like Victories, with wreaths and palms, though, unlike Victory, they remain naked; similarly, the dedications are in Latin. The education in Roman ways and Roman equivalents has thus begun which will eventually turn these folk or their sons into Roman citizens. At Longovicium (Lanchester, Co. Durham) the Suebi were worshipping their goddess Garmangabis. The Germans at Voreda (Old Penrith, Cumberland) imported the Unseni Fersomari, perhaps the most uncouth-sounding group that has survived. This permission to outlanders to retain their homeland cults has sometimes been interpreted as a barbarization of Roman religion; but the Romanizing tendency, by which barbaric cults were accepted, formulated, and shaped to Roman convention is no less important. So also is the frequent association of the dedications with the *numen Augusti*, stressing an Imperial loyalty. It was a Roman Empire and a Roman pantheon in which these deities took their place.

A more ambiguous northern cult, associated with both

the army and civilians, has left numerous dedications in the central and western areas of the zone of Hadrian's Wall. The name of the deity concerned is variously spelt and seems to have started as something like Hvitir; but it ends often as a plural, in the form Vitires or Vetires, so that, were it not for the ever inconsistent spelling, the dedicators might be thought to have intended their humble altars for the *di veteres*, 'the old gods'. Hvitir, with its initial aspirate, suggests a German origin; but the centre of the cult is unknown, and, while German irregular troops do appear in the area, at Castlesteads, it would be rash to connect them with this cult without further evidence.

Many of the western cults so far described were at a stage in which worship took the form of corporate vows rather than individual allegiances. The Eastern cults had a more developed basis of appeal and called for greater individual response. One of the most popular, especially in higher circles, was that of Iuppiter Dolichenus, the god of Doliche whose high seat was in Commagene, and who, with his consort Iuno Regina, made animal creation his footstool and the firmament of heaven his kingdom. He required for his worship a special form of temple, the Eastern house-type with many rooms, of which the existence in Britain is attested by various inscriptions. No British example has, however, yet been identified on the ground and excavated, although a fine sculptured frieze from such a building exists at Corbridge (Northumberland). His orders and advice were interpreted by the priest in charge of the temple, and it was no doubt his capacity to furnish responses to the perplexed that won for Dolichenus his popularity. To the army his appeal was also that of a powerful war-god and a great worker in iron for sinews of war. In Britain his worship first

occurs in the middle of the second century A.D., but
reaches its peak in the third. For a few years, indeed, the
Emperor Alexander Severus (A.D. 222–35) and the
Empress-Mother, Iulia Mamaea, were actually identified
with Dolichenus and his consort, and worshipped in that
guise in regimental headquarters, of which a relic seems
to exist in a statue at Chesters (Northumberland). Less
popular in the West was Iuppiter Heliopolitanus, whose
mightly temple at Heliopolis (Baalbeck) still proclaims
the wealth and influence of the cult in the Syrian world
to which it belonged. There is no doubt that the Roman
world was disgusted by the zeal with which the Syrian-
born Emperor Elagabalus (A.D. 218–22) plunged as high
priest into the most extreme forms of Heliopolitan worship, and this is probably the reason why it failed to rival
the less orgiastic cult of Dolichenus. Sometimes, on the
other hand, the direct association of an Emperor with a
cult seems to be the sole reason for its appearance in
Britain. The connexion of Severus with Serapis is the
likeliest explanation of the occurrence of a temple at
York, and of a Kirkby Thore (Westmorland) dedication:
it is certainly responsible for a Castlesteads gem, which
shows him in this guise. A parallel case is the compliment
to his Empress, Julia Domna, as Caelestis by the inclusion of this epithet, in word and representation, in the
personification of Brigantia, described above (p. 191). On
the other hand, it was a mistaken association with the
Emperor Commodus and the public obliteration of his
memory which led to the mutilation of a fine legionary
dedication to Sol Invictus, the Unconquered Sun-god, at
Corbridge (Northumberland) which had been set up in
A.D. 162–3. This form of sun-worship also came from the
East, but is rare in Britain, except when later associated
with that of Mithras. Rarer still is the cult of the Tyrian

Hercules and Astarte his consort at Corbridge, with its altars (now in London and Carlisle) dedicated in Greek. This was served by a priestess, and is probably connected with the known presence here of Eastern traders.

None of these Eastern cults appears to have been so highly organized as that of Mithras, the god of Persian and Zoroastrian origin whose cult reached Rome in the first century B.C. Mithras was a god who exacted from the individual worshipper high standards of conduct, probity, and courage, in exchange for an ultimate revelation and union. Knowledge of the mysteries, with their sacred symbolism, precepts, and ritual food and drink, was attained by grades of initiation, in which physical and psychological ordeals were included. For these reasons the cult was secret and it excluded women. It can be well understood how its tenets might appeal to a good soldier or an upright merchant; but to suppose that it had a wide appeal would be wrong. It asked too much effort, both spiritual and intellectual, in a religious climate where little was required. The suggestion conveyed by Rudyard Kipling, whose intuition so often enabled him to hit the mark, that Mithraism was a common religion, is belied both by the dedications and the size of Mithraic temples. The dedications are habitually made by officers and usually by commandants, while the temples in the military area are so small that they can never have held more than a dozen or at most a score of worshippers. The only temple yet known in the civilian area is the fine example in London, where a legionary veteran occurs among the wealthy merchant worshippers. Wherever they were erected, however, the temples always conformed to a standard type, in which the essential elements were the sanctuary, a long narrow nave flanked by single low solid benches facing out into it, and an outer room screened off from the nave. The heyday of the cult was undoubtedly the third and early fourth century A.D., and it is to this period that the excavated examples on Hadrian's Wall belong. Three are now known, at Borcovicium (Housesteads), Brocolitia (Carrawburgh), and Vindobala (Rudchester), the last being the largest, though the least well preserved. This is not the place for a detailed description, but interesting points emerge from comparison between the three. In the Rudchester and Carrawburgh temples the dedications were made by commandants of the regiment, who either introduced the cult or acted as its chief ministrants. At Housesteads the dedicators were a legionary centurion and a legionary seconded to special duties by the consular governor. It is evident that there was no long or regular succession of men capable of organizing the elaborate ritual, and at Carrawburgh and Housesteads there were indications of an intermittent use of the building punctu-ated by periods of disuse, when it was deserted though in no sense desecrated. All three temples were partly des-troyed by the barbarian invasion at the close of the third century A.D., but only Rudchester and Carrawburgh appear to have been rebuilt, while Housesteads remained devastated. The ultimate fate of Rudchester is not clear, but Carrawburgh was deliberately desecrated and thrown down fairly early in the fourth century A.D., its site being used henceforward as a rubbish dump for animal refuse. This looks like the work of a Christian commandant; for certain aspects of Mithraism, and especially the ritual meal, were regarded by Christians as a diabolical mock-ery of Christian sacraments. The different aspects of the cult should be noted. At Rudchester the accent in the dedi-cations is upon the sun-god who was the companion and adviser of Mithras, except upon one altar, of which the sculptured reliefs refer to two of the different grades. At Carrawburgh, the emphasis is upon Mithras. In one period of use stress was also placed upon initiation by ordeal, a cist for temporary entombment being provided. Revelation was later stressed, and a remarkable altar depicts the god as he is described in an Egyptian liturgy at the moment of his manifestation in glory, his sun-ray crown being pierced for illumination from behind. Comparable use of a sudden lighting-effect was made at Housesteads, where Mithras is given the title *saecularis* and is so portrayed, as Lord of Ages, in a pierced background of radiance enclosed by the signs of the Zodiac. It is possible that the different representational emphasis corresponds to differences in ritual, but in all the shrines Mithras and his two attendant gods of light and darkness are present, and at both Carrawburgh and Housesteads there is evidence for the existence of the central bull-killing relief, representing the conquest of wild nature and the release by Mithras of the vital forces from which sprang the good things of the earth. Whatever the variations in emphasis or presentation, it seems certain that the central tenets remained the same. One widespread misconception about the ritual should be removed. Although Mithras slew the bull, to release the vital power of the blood, his worshippers neither bathed nor were baptized in it. There is no evidence whatever for this practice, which belonged to the worship not of Mithras but of Cybele.

So complicated a ritual and theology explains why the cult of Mithras appealed to few. Yet its personal appeal secured those few, and often influential, initiates at many points. In addition to the three known temples, there is evidence for Mithraism on or near the Wall at Castlesteads and Carlisle, Newcastle, Wallsend, and High Rochester, while the fortresses at York, Chester, and Caerleon have also yielded good evidence for the practice of the cult in their midst. The London example, with its numerous associated deities, is linked with Eastern merchants as well as with a veteran, perhaps associated with the garrison of the provincial capital, quartered in the Cripplegate corner of the Roman city.

Of other mystery religions there is little trace in military contexts, though Corbridge has yielded some fragments of sculpture suggestive of the worship of Cybele. Here, as in the cult of Hercules and Astarte, such dedications may be due to immigrant traders rather than to military men. Christianity has yielded no trace at all, though a Gnostic gem from a signet-ring at Castlesteads may suggest the existence of a stray eclectic believer, just as there must have been stray Christians.

The religious life of the province was thus remarkably diverse, but from the Roman point of view there was rationality in the diversity. In Roman eyes the most important worship was that of the citizen body, corporately and individually. One of the reasons given for the extension of the citizenship in A.D. 213 was that there should thus be created more citizens to worship the gods, to whom the welfare and salvation of the State was due. While the evidence for regular calendared observances by Roman citizens in the British *coloniae* is weak, it is not absent; there is enough to make it quite certain that the requirements were regularly followed. The army, on the other hand, presents a remarkably orderly picture and its most remarkable side is not so much the Roman citizen army, of the legions, but the army of the auxiliary troops. While these men were not Roman citizens, they had nevertheless taken an oath of loyalty to Emperor and State, and their commandants were educated and wealthy Roman citizens. Such units worshipped the

Roman military gods corporately on the parade-ground and annual vows were paid both by the unit and by its commandant. But the matter did not end there: the military gods had their special festivals throughout the year, while members of the Imperial House, living and deified, were similarly honoured. All these feasts were duly and regularly observed, together with the more purely military functions, like the Rosaliae signorum or the Armilustrium. The troops would not take their part in such festivals without learning something of what they meant, either by observation or actual instruction, such as might come from an intelligent commandant, with the effect that slowly but surely these conscripts from frontier lands learnt the import of Roman religion and felt their way towards conscious and responsible membership of the Roman state. Until A.D. 213, Roman citizenship was granted to them on retirement after their twenty-five years service: after then, if they were born free within the Empire, it was theirs already and, although the old outward forms which distinguished the traditions of such regiments from those of the legions seem to have survived, they would take part in their traditional calendared festivals with a sense of still more immediate relevance.

The arrangements made for levies from the borders of the Empire, who supplemented the *auxilia* from the second century A.D. onwards, are less evident. It is clear that these troops were permitted to establish corporately their own native cults and that the dedications of such cults were usually coupled with vows to the *numen Augusti*. Roman loyalties were thus linked to memories of the homeland from the first. But it cannot be doubted that such troops also shared in at least the annual vows and the logical course would certainly have been to associate them, however distantly, with the general run of important festivals. They were destined ultimately to become citizens of the Empire and the sole question would be how rapidly understanding and sympathy in relation to its cults might be induced. It may well be that the first generation of men in such levies did not progress far beyond expressions of loyalty to the Imperial House. But in addition to this, it is important to observe how a Roman guise or interpretation is accorded to their native deities from the first, for this is in reality another and perhaps more subtle way of educating the worshipper.

Through the association of their own cults with an expression of reverence for the Emperor's *numen* the imported levies are in fact brought into line with natives of the province in general. It is clear that the opportunity for combining worship with a declaration of loyalty was regularly taken by provincials and it may be presumed that it was regularly expected of them. Otherwise there was evidently a wide diversity of cults, most of them harking back to pre-Roman days. It is difficult, however, to estimate whether such deities as the Matres were already indigenous to the province or whether they were introduced to Britain by Gauls from overseas during the Roman occupation. If these are eliminated, then the cults of the British province would appear to be considerably more localized than those of Gaul, or at least there is an absence of generally worshipped deities. This may well be true, for it would reflect the notable lack of political cohesion and cultural unity which permitted so rapid an acquisition of the province and defeated the first attempt to introduce a religious focus of loyalty at Camulodunum.

BIBLIOGRAPHY

This bibliography has been arranged chapter by chapter and in the order in which the subjects mentioned occur in each individual chapter.

LIST OF GENERAL WORKS UPON
ROMAN BRITAIN

F. Haverfield, *The Romanization of Roman Britain* (4th edition, Oxford, 1923).

F. Haverfield and Sir George Macdonald, *The Roman Occupation of Britain* (Oxford, 1924).

R. G. Collingwood, *Roman Britain* (Oxford, 1924).

R. G. Collingwood, *The Archaeology of Roman Britain* (London, 1930).

Ian Richmond, *Roman Britain* (London, 1947).

E. Birley, *Roman Britain and the Roman Army* (Kendal, 1953).

A. R. Burn, *Agricola and Roman Britain* (London, 1953).

J. Ward, *Romano-British Buildings and Earthworks* (London, 1911).

CHAPTER I

MILITARY HISTORY

C. E. Stevens, 'Britain between the invasions (54 B.C.–A.D. 43)'. *Aspects of Archaeology in Britain and beyond* (1951).

G. C. Brooke, 'The Distribution of Gaulish and British coins in Britain', *Antiquity*, vii (1933), 268–89.

D. Allen, 'The Belgic Dynasties of Britain and their coins', *Archaeologia*, xc (1944), 1–46.

C. F. C. Hawkes and M. R. Hull, 'Camulodunum', *Reports of the Research Committee of the Society of Antiquaries of London*, xiv (1947).

T. Davies Pryce, 'The Roman occupation of Britain: its early phase', *Antiquaries Journal*, xviii (1938), 29–48.

R. E. M. and T. V. Wheeler, 'Verulamium, a Belgic and two Roman cities'; *Reports of the Research Committee of the Society of Antiquaries of London*, xi (1936).

C. F. C. Hawkes and G. C. Dunning, 'The Belgae of Gaul and Britain', *Archaeological Journal*, lxxxvii (1930), 150–335.

C. F. C. Hawkes, 'Hill-forts', *Antiquity* v (1931), 60–97.

J. P. Bushe-Fox, 'Fourth Report on the excavations of the Roman fort at Richborough, Kent'; *Reports of the Research Committee of the Society of Antiquaries of London*, xvi (1949).

R. E. M. Wheeler, 'Maiden Castle, Dorset', *Reports of the Research Committee of the Society of Antiquaries of London*, xii (1943).

Hod Hill: O. G. S. Crawford and A. Keiller, *Wessex from the Air* (Oxford, 1928), 31–46.

C. F. C. Hawkes, 'Britons, Romans, and Saxons round Salisbury and in Cranborne Chase', *Archaeological Journal*, civ, 27–81.

Sir Cyril Fox, *A find of the Early Iron Age from Llyn Cerrig Bach, Anglesey* (Cardiff, Nat. Museum, 1946).

E. Birley, 'The epitaph of Iulius Classicianus', *Antiquaries Journal*, xvi (1936), 207–8.

S. N. Miller, 'Roman York', *Journal of Roman Studies*, xv (1925), 176–94; xviii (1928), 61–99.

P. Corder, 'The Defences of the Roman fort at Malton', *Roman Malton and District Report no. 2* (Yorkshire Archaeological Society).

I. A. Richmond and G. Webster, 'Excavations in Goss Street, Chester, 1948–9', *Journal of the Chester Archaeological Society*, xxxviii (1950), 1–38.

G. Webster, 'Excavations on the legionary defences at Chester, 1949–52', *Journal of the Chester Archaeological Society*, xl (1953), 1–23.

I. A. Richmond and J. McIntyre, 'The Roman camps at Rey Cross and Crackenthorpe', *Cumberland and Westmorland Antiquarian and Archaeological Society's Transactions*, N.S., xxxiv (1934), 50–61.

V. E. Nash-Williams, *The Roman frontier in Wales* (Cardiff, 1954).

Sir George Macdonald, 'The Agricolan occupation of North Britain', *Journal of Roman Studies*, ix (1919), 111–38.

S. N. Miller, 'The fifth campaign of Agricola', *Journal of Roman Studies*, xxxviii (1948), 15–19.

I. A. Richmond, 'Gnaeus Julius Agricola', *Journal of Roman Studies*, xxxiv (1944), 34–45.

J. Curle, *A Roman frontier-post and its people* (Glasgow, 1911).

I. A. Richmond, 'Excavations at the Roman fort of Newstead, 1947', *Proceedings of the Society of Antiquaries of Scotland*, lxxxiv (1950), 1–38.

Tassiesholm, Journal of Roman Studies, xli (1951), 123.

I. A. Richmond and J. K. St Joseph, 'The Roman fort at Glenlochar, Kirkcudbrightshire', *Transactions of the Dumfriesshire and Galloway Nat. Hist. and Ant. Soc.*, xxx (1953).

J. K. St Joseph, 'Air reconnaissance of North Britain', *Journal of Roman Studies*, xli (1951), 52–65.

I. A. Richmond and J. McIntyre, 'The Agricolan fort at Fendoch', *Proceedings of the Society of Antiquaries of Scotland*, lxxiii (1939), 110–54.

Corbridge: see *Archaeologia Aeliana*, 4th series, vols. xi, xv, xvii, xxi, xxviii, xxx, xxxi.

J. Collingwood Bruce, *Handbook to the Roman Wall*, 10th edition (Newcastle upon Tyne, 1947).

E. Birley, *The Centenary Pilgrimage of Hadrian's Wall* (1949).

F. G. Simpson and I. A. Richmond, 'The Turf Wall of Hadrian, 1895–1935', *Journal of Roman Studies*, xxv (1934), 1–18.

I. A. Richmond, 'Hadrian's Wall, 1939–49', *Journal of Roman Studies*, xl (1950), 43–56.

Sir George Macdonald, *The Antonine Wall in Scotland* (2nd edition, Oxford, 1934).

J. P. Gillam, 'Calpurnius Agricola and the northern frontier', *Trans. Architectural and Archaeological Society of Durham and Northumberland*, x (1953), 359–75.

S. N. Miller, 'Severus in Britain', *Cambridge Ancient History*, xii, 36–42.

I. A. Richmond, 'The Romans in Redesdale', *Northumberland County History*, xv, 63–159.

J. P. Bushe-Fox, 'Some notes on Roman coast defences', *Journal of Roman Studies*, xxii (1932), 60–72.

W. Hornsby and J. D. Laverick, 'The Roman signal-station at Goldsborough, near Whitby, Yorks', *Archaeological Journal*, lxxxix (1933), 203–19; M. R. Hull, 'The pottery from the Roman signal-stations on the Yorkshire coast', *ibid.* 220–53.

P. H. Blair, *The origins of Northumbria* (Newcastle upon Tyne, 1948).

J. N. L. Myres, 'The Adventus Saxonum', *Aspects of Archaeology in Britain and beyond* (1951), 221–41.

CHAPTER 2

TOWNS AND URBAN CENTRES

A. Fox, *Roman Exeter* (Manchester Univ. Press, 1952).

S. Frere, 'Canterbury Excavations', *Antiquity*, xxiii (1949), 153–60.

K. M. Kenyon, 'Excavations at the Jewry Wall site, Leicester', *Reports of the Research Committee of the Society of Antiquaries of London*, xv (1948).

R. E. M. and T. V. Wheeler, 'Verulamium, a Belgic and two Roman cities', *Reports of the Research Committee of the Society of Antiquaries of London*, xi (1936).

A. W. G. Lowther, 'Report on excavations at Verulamium in 1934',
   Antiquaries Journal, xvii (1937), 28–51.

K. M. Kenyon, 'The Roman theatre at Verulamium, St Albans',
   Archaeologia, lxxxiv (1935), 213–61.

K. M. Richardson, 'Report on Excavations at Verulamium, Insula
   xvii, 1938', *Archaeologia*, xc (1944), 81–126.

I. A. Richmond, 'The four coloniae of Roman Britain', *Archaeological
   Journal*, ciii (1947), 57–84.

I. A. Richmond, 'The Roman city of Lincoln', *Archaeological Journal*,
   ciii (1947), 26–56.

R. E. M. Wheeler, *London in Roman times* (London Museum Cata-
   logues, no. 3), London, 1930.

Royal Commission on Historical Monuments (England), An inventory of the historical monuments in London, iii, *Roman London*.
   H.M. Stationery Office, 1928.

London, Roman fort at Cripplegate, Journal of Roman Studies, xl (1950),
   108; xli (1951), 134.

J. P. Bushe-Fox, 'Excavations on the site of the Roman town at
   Wroxeter, Shropshire, in 1912; 1913; 1914', *Reports of the
   Research Committee of the Society of Antiquaries of London*, nos. i, ii,
   and iv.

G. C. Dunning, 'Two fires of Roman London', *Antiquaries Journal*,
   xxv (1945), 48–77.

D. Atkinson, *Report on Excavations at Wroxeter (the Roman city of
   Viroconium) in the County of Salop, 1923–7* (Oxford, 1942).

Venta Icenorum: Journal of Roman Studies, xix (1929), 196; xxi (1931),
   232–3; xxii (1932), 210; xxiv (1934), 209–10; xxv (1935), 213;
   xxvi (1936), 251; xxix (1939), 214.

V. E. Nash-Williams, 'The forum and basilica and public baths of the
   Roman town of Venta Silurum at Caerwent in Monmouthshire',
   Bulletin of the Board of Celtic Studies, xv (1953), 159–67.

Ministry of Works, *Caerwent Roman City, Monmouthshire* (H.M.
   Stationery Office, 1951).

P. Corder and I. A. Richmond, 'Petuaria', *Journal of British Archaeological Association*, Ser. 3, vii (1942), 1–30.

Isurium Brigantum, H. Eckroyd Smith, *Reliquiae Isurianae* (London,
   1852): *Journal of Roman Studies*, xxv (1934), 205–6; xxvi (1936),
   244; xxviii (1938), 178–9; xxix (1939), 204.

E. Birley, 'Housesteads, the civil settlement', *Archaeologia Aeliana*,
   4th series, xii (1935), 205–46.

Air-photographs of vici at forts, Journal of Roman Studies, xli (1951), 53–5.

A. O. Curle, 'Description of the fortifications on Ruberslaw, Roxburghshire, and notices of Roman remains found there', *Proceedings of the Society of Antiquaries of Scotland*, xxxix (1905), 219–32.

K. A. Steer and R. W. Feachem, 'A Roman signal-station on Eildon
Hill North, Roxburghshire', *Proceedings of the Society of Antiquaries
of Scotland*, lxxxvi, 202–5.

Victoria County History, Hampshire, i, F. Haverfield, *Silchester*,
271–84; G. E. Fox and Sir W. H. St John Hope, *The Romano-
British Town of Calleva Atrebatum, at Silchester*, 350–72.

M. A. Cotton, 'Excavations at Silchester, 1938–9', *Archaeologia*, xcii
(1947), 121–67.

F. Haverfield, 'Bath', *Victoria County History, Somerset*, i, 219–88.

W. H. Knowles, 'The Roman Baths at Bath', *Archaeologia*, lxxv(1924–
5), 1–17.

F. Haverfield, 'Buxton', *Victoria County History, Derbyshire*, 1, 222–7.

G. H. Jack and A. G. K. Hayter, *Excavations on the site of the Romano-
British town of Magna, Kenchester, Herefordshire*, ii (1924–5); (The
Woolhope Naturalists' Field Club): J. K. St Joseph, *Journal of
Roman Studies*, xliii (1953), pl. xiv, 1.

D. B. Harden, 'Alchester', *Victoria County History, Oxfordshire*, i, 281–8.

D. B. Harden, 'Dorchester on Thames', *Victoria County History, Oxfordshire*, i, 288–96.

A. H. A. Hogg and C. E. Stevens, 'The Defences of Roman Dorchester', *Oxoniensia*, ii (1937), 41–73.

C. D. Drew and K. C. Collingwood Selby, 'The Excavations at
Colliton Park, Dorchester, 1937–8, 1938', *Dorset Natural History
and Archaeological Society Journal*, lix, lx.

C. F. C. Hawkes, 'Roman Ancaster, Horncastle, and Caistor',
Archaeological Journal, ciii (1947), 17–25.

Dorchester aqueduct, K. M. Richardson, 'Excavations at Poundbury,
Dorchester, Dorset, 1939', *Antiquaries Journal*, xx (1940), 435–40.

Aesica Aqueduct, *Journal of Roman Studies*, xxxv (1945), 80.

Sir George Macdonald, 'Note on some fragments of Imperial statues
and of a statuette of victory', *Journal of Roman Studies*, xvi (1926),
1–16.

Sul Minerva, I. A. Richmond, *Roman Britain* (London, 1947), 31.

I. A. Richmond, 'An Imperial head of Constantine from York',
Antiquaries Journal, xxiv (1944), 1–5.

B. H. St J. O'Neil, 'The Silchester region in the fifth and sixth
centuries A.D.', *Antiquity*, xviii (1944), 113–22.

London Dykes: R. E. M. Wheeler, *London and the Saxons* (London
Museum Catalogue, no. 3), 28: 'London and the Grim's ditches',
Antiquaries Journal, xiv (1934), 254–63.

CHAPTER 3

THE COUNTRYSIDE

H. E. O'Neil, 'The Roman villa at Park Street, near St Albans, Hertfordshire', *Archaeological Journal*, cii (1945), 21–110.

J. B. Ward Perkins, 'The Roman villa at Lockleys', *Antiquaries Journal*, xviii (1938), 339–76.

C. A. R. Radford, 'The Roman site at Catsgore, Somerton', *Proceedings of the Somersetshire Archaeological and Natural History Society*, xcvi (1951), 41–77.

Philip Corder and John L. Kirk, 'A Roman Villa at Langton, near Malton, E. Yorkshire' (Roman Malton and District Report no. 4), *Yorkshire Archaeological Society*, 1932.

C. A. Ralegh Radford, 'The Roman villa at Ditchley, Oxon', *Oxoniensia*, i, 1936, 24–69; *Victoria County History, Oxfordshire*, i, 311–12.

Little Milton, Journal of Roman Studies, xl (1950), pl. vi, 2.

Clanville, Victoria County History, Hampshire and the Isle of Wight, 295–7; *Archaeologia*, iv (1898), 2–6.

Denton, Journal of Roman Studies, xl (1950), 100; William Fowler, *Engravings of the principal Mosaic Pavements which have been discovered . . . in various parts of Great Britain, etc.* (1804), pls. 9, 10.

Castlefield, Victoria County History, Hampshire and the Isle of Wight, i, 302.

S. E. Winbolt, *Roman Folkestone* (1925); *Victoria County History, Kent*, iii, 114–15.

Samuel Lysons, *Roman Antiquities at Woodchester* (1797); *Reliquiae Britannico-Romanae*, ii (1813), part i.

Northleigh, Victoria County History, Oxfordshire, i, 316–18.

V. E. Nash-Williams, 'The Roman Villa at Llantwit Major in Glamorgan', *Archaeologia Cambrensis*, cii (1953), 89–163.

Chedworth, G. E. Fox, 'Notes on some probable traces of Roman Fulling in Britain, *Archaeologia*, lix (1905), 210–4; *Titsey, ibid.*, 214–18. *Darenth, ibid.*, 214–18.

Darenth, G. Payne, 'The Roman Villa at Darenth', *Archaeologia Cantiana*, xxii (1896), 49–84; *Victoria County History, Kent*, iii, 111–13.

A. H. Cocks, 'A Romano-British Homestead in the Hambleden Valley, Bucks', *Archaeologia*, lxxi (1921), 140–98.

A. M. Woodward, 'The Roman Villa at Rudston, Yorkshire', *Archaeological Journal*, xxxi (1934), 366–76; xxxii (1936), 214–20; with K. A. Steer, xxxiii (1938), 81–6; K. A. Steer, *ibid.*, 321–38.

I. A. Richmond, T. Romans, R. P. Wright, 'A civilian Bath-house of the Roman Period at Old Durham, *Archaeologia Aeliana*, 4th series, xxii (1944), 1–21; R. P. Wright and J. P. Gillam, 'Second Report on Roman Buildings at Old Durham', *ibid.*, xxix (1951), 203–12: 'Third Report', *ibid.*, xxxi (1953), 116–26.

Professor Buckman and C. H. Newmarch, *Remains of Roman Art in Cirencester . . . ancient Corinium* (London, 1850).

A. Fox, 'The date of the Orpheus mosaic', *Transactions of the Bristol and Gloucester Archaeological Society*, lxx (1951), 51–3.

H. Eckroyd Smith, *Reliquiae Isurianae* (1852); *A Roman Mosaic Pavement* (1867).

I. A. Richmond, *The Roman Pavements at Rudston*, 1935.

Lenthay Green mosaic, Royal Commission on Historical Monuments (England), *Report on West Dorset* (1952), 199, pl. 127.

Low Ham mosaic, Somerset Arch. and Nat. Hist. Soc. Proceedings, xcii (1916), 5–8; *Journal of Roman Studies*, xxxvi (1946), 142, pl. xi.

B. W. Pearce, 'Roman Site at Otford', *Archaeologia Cantiana*, xxxix (1927), 153; *Victoria County History*, Kent, iii, 122; *Journal of Roman Studies*, xvi (1926).

G. W. Meates, E. Greensfield, E. Birchenough, 'The Lullingstone Roman Villa', *Archaeologia Cantiana*, lxiii (1951), 1–49; *Journal of Roman Studies*, x (1950), 111–13, pl. xi.

J. E. and F. G. Hilton Price, *Remains of Roman Buildings at Morton near Brading* (London, 1887); *Victoria County History, Hampshire and the Isle of Wight*, i, 313–16.

Victoria County History, Leicestershire, i, 188–97.

Bramdean Mosaic, Victoria County History, Hampshire and the Isle of Wight, i, 307–8.

William Fowler, *Engravings of the principal Mosaic Pavements which have been discovered . . . in various parts of Great Britain, etc.* (1804), pl. 2.

R. Hinks, *Catalogue of the Greek, Etruscan, and Roman Paintings and Mosaics in the British Museum* (1933), 101–9, no. 36a–p.

Gosbecks, Journal of Roman Studies, xxvii (1937), 240; xxxviii (1948), 91; xxxix (1949), 106.

M. V. Taylor, 'Woodeaton', *Journal of Roman Studies*, vii (1917), 98–119; xxi (1931), 101–9; *Victoria County History*, Oxfordshire, i, 299–301; J. R. Kirk, 'Bronzes from Woodeaton, Oxon', *Oxoniensia*, xiv (1949), 1–45.

loca, I. A. Richmond and O. G. S. Crawford, 'The British section of the Ravenna Cosmography', *Archaeologia*, xciii, 15.

R. E. M. and T. V. Wheeler, 'Report on the excavation of the Pre-historic, Roman, and post-Roman site in Lydney Park, Gloucestershire, *Reports of the Research Committee of the Society of Antiquaries of London*, ix (1932).

C. E. Stevens, 'A possible conflict of laws in Roman Britain', *Journal of Roman Studies*, xxxvii (1947), 132–4.

C. F. C. Hawkes, 'Britons, Romans, and Saxons round Salisbury and in Cranborne Chase', *Archaeological Journal*, civ (1948), 1–48.

F. C. Payne, 'The plough in ancient Britain', *Archaeological Journal*, civ, 82–111.

F. Haverfield, 'Centuriation in Roman Essex', *Essex Archaeological Society Transactions*, xv (1921), 115–25.

J. G. D. Clark, 'Report on excavations on the Cambridgeshire Car Dyke, 1947', *Antiquaries Journal*, xxix (1949), 145–63.

Villages, Royal Commission on Historical Monuments (England), *An Inventory of the historical monuments in Westmorland*, p. xxxii, ff. (1936).

R. G. Collingwood, 'Prehistoric settlements near Crosby Ravensworth', *Cumberland and Westmorland Antiquarian and Archaeological Society's Trans.*, N.S. xxxiii (1933), 201–26.

A. Raistrick, 'Iron-Age settlements in West Yorkshire', *Yorkshire Archaeological Journal*, xxxiv (1939), 115–50; *Journal of Roman Studies*, xl (1950), pl. vi, 1.

Gargrave, R. Rauthmel, *Antiquitates Bremetonacenses or The Roman Antiquities of Overborough* (2nd edition, Kirby Lonsdale, 1824), 16–17.

I. A. Richmond, 'The Sarmatae, Bremetannacum Veteranorum and the regio Bremetennacensis', *Journal of Roman Studies*, xxxv (1945), 15–29.

Lake-dwellings, V. G. Childe, *The Prehistory of Scotland*, 211–12.

R. E. M. Wheeler, 'A Romano-Celtic temple near Harlow, Essex, and a note on the type', *Antiquaries Journal*, viii (1928), 300–26.

J. S. P. Bradford and R. G. Goodchild, 'Excavations at Frilford, Berkshire, 1937–8', *Oxoniensia*, iii, 1–70.

Titsey Temple, *Journal of Roman Studies*, xxvi (1936), 262–3.

Nettleton Scrub, F. Haverfield, *Roman Britain in 1913* (British Academy Supplemental Papers, ii), 49.

Barkway, British Museum: *Guide to the Antiquities of Roman Britain in the Department of British and Medieval Antiquities*, 34–5; *Victoria County History, Hertfordshire*, i (1914), 148, pl. x.

Stony Stratford, British Museum: Guide to the Antiquities of Roman Britain in the Department of British and Medieval Antiquities (1953), 36.

Vinotonus, *Journal of Roman Studies*, xxxvi (1946), 146; xxxvii (1947), 179.

G. C. Dunning and R. F. Jessup, 'Roman Barrows', *Antiquity*, x (1936), 37–53.

Walled cemeteries, *Victoria County History, Kent*, iii, 94, pl. xiv.

Mersea, Royal Commission on Historical Monuments (England), *Essex (North-East)*, 229–30.

Harpenden, *St Albans and Hertfordshire Architectural and Archaeological Society Transactions* (1937), 108.

J. P. Bushe-Fox, 'Fourth Report on the Excavations of the Roman fort at Richborough, Kent'; *Reports of the Research Committee of the Society of Antiquaries of London*, xvi (1949), 38–48.

I. A. Richmond and R. P. Wright, 'Stones from a Hadrianic war memorial on Tyneside', *Archaeologia Aeliana*, 4th series, xxi, 93–120.

Hawkshaw, J. Curle, 'An inventory of objects of Roman and provincial Roman origin found on sites in Scotland not definitely associated with Roman constructions', *Proceedings of the Society of Antiquaries of Scotland*, lxvi (1931–2), 326–9.

CHAPTER 4

ECONOMICS

R. G. Collingwood, 'Roman Britain', in *An Economic Survey of Ancient Rome*, iii, 1–118.

R. G. Collingwood, 'Roman Britain', chapter iv, *Mining and minerals*, *An Economic Survey of Ancient Rome*, iii.

O. Davies, *Roman mines in Europe* (Oxford, 1935); *The British Isles*, 140–64.

G. C. Whittick, 'Roman mining in Britain', *Transactions of the Newcomen Society*, xii (1931–2), 57–79.

J. A. Smythe, 'Roman pigs of lead from Brough', *Transactions of the Newcomen Society*, xx (1939–40), 139–45.

I. A. Richmond, 'Roman leaden sealings from Brough-under-Stainmore', *Cumberland and Westmorland Antiquarian and Archaeological Society Transactions*, N.S., xxxvi (1936), 104–25.

J. A. Smythe, 'Roman objects of copper and iron from the north of England', *Proceedings of the University of Durham Philosophical Society*, ix (1938), Appendix, *Paraffin wax*, 400–1.

Machen, V. E. Nash-Williams, *Archaeologia Cambrensis*, xciv (1939), 108.

O. Davies, 'The copper mines on Great Orme's Head, Caernarvonshire', *Archaeologia Cambrensis*, c (1948), 61–6.

Anglesey copper: Royal Commission on Ancient Monuments, Wales, *Anglesey*, Appendices III and IV, pp. lxxxvi-xc.

V. E. Nash-Williams, 'The Roman gold-mines at Dolaucothi (Carm.)', *Bulletin of the Board of Celtic Studies*, xiv (1950), 79–84.

O. Davies, 'Finds at Dolaucothy', *Archaeologia Cambrensis*, xci (1936), 51–7.

Corbridge iron-working, *Archaeologia Aeliana*, 3rd series, viii, 207–9.

Coal, R. G. Collingwood, *Economic Survey of Ancient Rome*, iii, 35–7.

Kimmeridge shale, British Museum Guide to the Antiquities of Roman Britain (1922), 69–71; *Journal of Roman Studies*, xxii (1932), 206–7.

Purbeck Marble, G. C. Dunning, *Archaeological News-letter*, March, 1949, 15.

Jet and gypsum, I. A. Richmond, 'The four *coloniae* of Roman Britain', *Archaeological Journal*, ciii (1947), 79.

M. Steuart, 'Scots pearls', *Scottish Historical Review*, xvii (1920), 287–95.

Cropping shears, *Archaeological Journal*, xiii, 10, pl. 3, no. 30.

Dye-works, Silchester, *Archaeologia*, liv, 459–67: *Victoria County History, Hampshire*, i, 353.

E. T. Artis, *The Durobrivae of Antoninus, etc.*, London, 1828.

Heywood Sumner, *New Forest Pottery Sites* (1927).

H. M. Callender, 'Amphora stamps from Corbridge', *Archaeologia Aeliana*, 4th series, xxvii (1949), 60–117.

A. W. G. Lowther, *A survey of the prehistory of the Farnham district*, part iii (Surrey Archaeological Society, 1939), 221 ff.

W. F. Grimes, 'Pottery and Tilery of the XXth Legion at Holt', *Cymmrodorion Society Transactions*, 1930.

Knapton pottery, P. Corder and J. L. Kirk, *The Roman villa at Langton* (Roman Malton and District Report, no. 3), 96.

P. Corder, 'The Roman pottery at Crambeck, Castle Howard', *Roman Malton and District Report no. 1* (1928).

P. Corder, 'A pair of fourth-century Romano-British pottery kilns near Crambeck, with a note on the dsitribution of Crambeck ware, by Margaret Birley', *Antiquaries Journal*, xvii (1937), 392–413.

A. W. G. Lowther, 'A Study of the patterns on Roman flue-tiles and their distribution', *Research papers of the Surrey Archaeological Society*, no. 1 (1948).

Plaxtol tiles, F. Haverfield, *Proceedings of the Society of Antiquaries of London*, xxiii (1911), 109.

I. A. Richmond, 'Part of the stem of a Roman monumental candelabrum of stone, from York', *Antiquaries Journal*, xxvi (1946), 1–10.

Capheaton paterae, British Museum Guide to the Antiquities of Roman Britain (1922), 90–3.

R. C. Bosanquet, 'A Roman skillet from South Shields', *Archaeologia Aeliana*, 4th series, xiii (1936), 139–51.

Colchester Samian pottery, M. R. Hull, *Germania*, xviii (1934), 27–36.

G. Simpson, 'The Aldgate potter, a maker of Romano-British Samian ware', *Journal of Roman Studies*, xlii (1952), 68–71.

Glass: I. A. Richmond, 'The four *coloniae* of Roman Britain', *Archaeological Journal*, ciii (1947), 80.

Marble imported, *Journal of Roman Studies*, xii (1922), 221.

C. H. V. Sutherland, *Coinage and currency in Roman Britain* (Oxford, 1937).

C. H. V. Sutherland, 'Romano-British imitations of bronze coins of Claudius I', *Numismatic Notes and Monographs*, no. 65 (New York, 1935).

B. H. St J. O'Neil, 'A hoard of late Roman coins from Northamptonshire; its parallels and significance', *Archaeological Journal*, xc, 282–305.

CHAPTER 5

RELIGIONS

Colchester: Royal Commission on Historical Monuments (England) *Essex* (*North-East*), 24–6: cf. *Journal of Roman Studies*, ix (1919), 146.

Jupiter-column: F. Haverfield, *Archaeologia*, lxix (1920), 188–91.

Chichester inscription: Tacitus, *Agricola*, Furneaux and Anderson (Oxford, 1922), 79, fig. 10.

Silchester Tutela, *Victoria County History*, *Hampshire*, i, 363.

Segomo, *Victoria County History*, *Hampshire*, i, 280, fig. 7.

Matres, F. Haverfield, *Archaeologia*, lxix (1920), 181.

Nutrices; *Archaeologia*, lxix (1920), 183–4.

Cybele, R. E. M. and T. V. Wheeler, 'Verulamium, a Belgic and two Roman cities', *Reports of the Research Committee of the Society of Antiquaries of London*, xi (1936), 113–20.

Brigantia, N. Jolliffe, *Archaeological Journal*, xcviii (1941), 36–61.

P. Corder and I. A. Richmond, 'A Romano-British interment, with bucket and sceptres, from Brough, East Yorkshire', *Antiquaries Journal*, xviii (1938), 68–74.

Ocelus, V. E. Nash-Williams, *Bulletin of the Board of Celtic Studies*, xv (1951), 83–8.

Silchester temple Archaeologia, liv, Report for 1893.

Verulamium temple, *Antiquaries Journal*, xvii (1937), 28–51.

Gosbecks temple-site, *Journal of Roman Studies*, xl (1950), 108.

Gosbecks Mercury, *Journal of Roman Studies*, xxxviii (1948), pl. xiv.

Mars Medocius, *Archaeological Journal*, xlix, 213–19.

Rigisamus, R. G. Collingwood, *Proceedings of the Somersetshire Archaeological and Natural History Society*, lxxvii (1931), 112–14.

Leucetius, *Victoria County History*, *Somerset*, i, 272.

R. E. M. Wheeler, 'Maiden Castle, Dorset', *Reports of the Research Committee of the Society of Antiquaries of London*, xii (1943), 131–4.

Ancasta, *Victoria County History*, *Hampshire*, i, 336.

N. F. Layard, 'Bronze crowns and a bronze head-dress from a Roman site on Cavenham Heath, Suffolk', *Antiquaries Journal*, v (1925), 258–65.

Antenociticus, I. A. Richmond, *Archaeologia Aeliana*, 4th series, xix (1941), 37–9.

Coventina, *Archaeologia Aeliana*, 2nd series, viii (1880), 1–49.

Maponus, I. A. Richmond, *Archaeologia Aeliana*, 4th series, xxi (1943), 206–10.

Cocidius, I. A. Richmond and J. McIntyre, *Archaeologia Aeliana*, 4th series, xiv (1937), 103–9.

Belatucadrus, *Transactions of the Cumberland and Westmorland Antiquarian and Archaeological Society*, N.S., xxxii, 136–7.

Contrebis, E. Birley, *Cumberland and Westmorland Antiquarian and Archaeological Society's Transactions*, N.S., xlvi (1947), 135–7.

Verbeia, *Corpus Inscriptionum Latinarum*, vii, 208.

Setlocenia, K. Jackson, *Language and History in Early Britain* (1953), 325.

Vanauns, *Transactions of the Cumberland and Westmorland Antiquarian and Archaeological Society*, N.S., xxii, 209.

Oceanus, *Northumberland County History*, xiii, 512–13, 543–5.

Earith statue, *Victoria County History*, *Huntingdonshire* (1926), 264.

Ranksborough Jupiter, *British Museum Guide to the Antiquities of Roman Britain* (1951), pl. xvi.

Nero; British Museum Guide to the Antiquities of Roman Britain (1951), pl. xiv.

Capheaton paterae, *British Museum Guide to the Antiquities of Roman Britain* (1922), 90–3.

Backworth hoard, *British Museum Guide to the Antiquities of Roman Britain* (1922), 62–3.

Mithras, London, *Journal of Roman Studies*, ii, 143 (older discovery).

Lullingstone, *Archaeologia Cantiana*, lxiii (1951), 1–49.

F. Haverfield, 'Early British Christianity', *English Historical Review*, xi (1896), 417–30.

F. Haverfield, *Catalogue of the Roman inscribed and sculptured stones in the Grosvenor Museum, Chester*, Chester, 1900.

Victory, *Journal of Roman Studies*, xvi (1926), 9–11.

Feriale Duranum, *Yale Classical Studies*, vii (1940), 1–222.

Disciplina, I. A. Richmond, *Archaeologia Aeliana*, 4th series, xxi (1943), 165–9.

Maryport altars; L. P. Wenham, *Transactions of the Cumberland and Westmorland Antiquarian and Archaeological Society*, N.S., xxxix (1939), 19–30.

Armilustrium, *Yale Classical Studies*, vii (1940), 163, 287.

Clarian Apollo, *Germania*, xxiii (1939) 189–90.

E. Birley, 'Marcus Cocceius Firmus, an epigraphic study', *Proceedings of the Society of Antiquaries of Scotland*, lxx (1935–6), 363–77.

Minerva, *Archaeologia Aeliana*, 4th series, xxi, 154–5.

Ollototae, F. Haverfield, *Archaeologia Aeliana*, 2nd series, xv (1892), 225–7.

Anextlomarus, *Archaeological Journal*, xlv, 171.

Thinesus, *Archaeologia Aeliana*, 2nd series, x, 148–70; *Archaeologia Aeliana*, 3rd series, xix (1922), 185–97.

Garmangabis; *Archaeologia Aeliana*, 2nd series, xvi, 313–27.

Unseni Fersomari, *Transactions of the Cumberland and Westmorland Antiquarian and Archaeological Society*, N.S., xi, 470–2.

F. Haverfield, 'Early Northumbrian Christianity and the altars to the *Di Veteres*', *Archaeologia Aeliana*, 3rd series, xv, 22–43.

Dolichenus, *Archaeologia Aeliana*, 4th series, xxi (1943), 179–93.

R. C. Bosanquet, 'Excavations at Housesteads; the temple of Mithras', *Archaeologia Aeliana*, 2nd series, xxv (1904), 255–63.

I. A. Richmond, J. P. Gillam, and E. Birley, 'The Temple of Mithras at Carrawburgh', *Archaeologia Aeliana*, 4th series, xxix (1951), 1–92.

INDEX